50
WEST CENTRAL
COLORADO
HIKING TRAILS

by Don and Roberta Lowe

The Touchstone Press
P.O. Box 81
Beaverton, Oregon 97005

Library of Congress Catalog Card No. 76-661

I.S.B.N. No. 0-911518-39-8

Maps courtesy of
U. S. Geological Survey

INTRODUCTION

One special delight for the Colorado hiker is the differing zones of vegetation he usually passes through during a trip. Many trails begin in aspen groves and, as the elevation increases, evergreens, such as lodgepole pine and spruce, begin to replace the less-hardy deciduous growth. Around 10,000 feet you leave what is called the Canadian zone and, until timberline—near 11,500 feet—travel through the Hudsonian zone of scattered spruce, fir and pine. The arctic-alpine zone above the tree line is a spartan, invigorating scene of low-growing grasses and other plants.

The wild flowers, for which the Colorado Rockies are most justifiably famous, also change with the zones and you will not have to make many hikes to begin anticipating some of the blooms you are certain to see—columbine is especially impressive beneath the aspen; marsh marigold thrives in the wet areas of the Hudsonian zone and the untypically robust alpine sunflower adds a big splash of yellow to the slopes above timberline.

Similarily, animal and bird life differs with the elevation. Porcupines waddle through the deep woods, conies and marmots prefer the higher rocky areas of the Hudsonian zone and ptarmigan blend with the colors of the tundra.

The 50 trails described in this guide explore terrain on the western slopes of the Rockies within an area bordered by Colorado 133 on the west, Interstate 70 and U.S. 6 on the north, U.S. 24 and the summit of the Sawatch Range on the east and the crest of the divide that forms the boundary of the White River and Gunnison National Forests on the south. Less precisely delineated, the region mostly is within the area formed by drawing a line south from Glenwood Springs to Marble then east to Independence Pass, north to Vail and west back to Glenwood Springs.

Just over one-half of the hikes end at lakes, six go to peaks, ten stop at passes and the remaining terminate at such interesting destinations as a cave, a mine and a hot springs.

The trails are grouped into areas in the Table of Contents so you immediately can determine the other hikes starting nearby. The beginning of the text for the first hike in each area is devoted to a brief summary of the trips in that section — whether the trailheads are the same, possible loops, how the routes differ in character, etc.

Hike No. 1 to Hanging Lake begins a short distance east of Glenwood Springs and is a contrast to the alpine scene experienced on the remaining 49 treks. No's. 2 and 3 probe the west side of the Gore Range and begin just six miles east of Vail. Trip No's. 4 through 7 originate in the Fulford area south of Eagle, a town midway between Vail and Glenwood Springs on I-170. Fulford is one of the several ghost mining towns visited by trails in this guide. The next two areas include trips that explore the Holy Cross (No's. 8 through 10) and Homestake Creek (No's. 11 through 16) areas just southwest of Vail. The Fryingpan River feeds Ruedi Reservoir and the eastern portion of the drainage is the locale for hikes No's. 17 through 22. This area is reached from Basalt, situated between Glenwood Springs and Aspen. A closer look at massive Mount Sopris, southeast of Glenwood Springs, is provided at the destinations of No's. 23 and 24. The region near the headwaters of the Crystal River was especially famous for the quality of its marble and hikes No's. 25 through 29 traverse the slopes of this region, including a fascinating visit to the marble quarry. Nine trails begin a short distance south of Aspen: No's. 32 through 36 start from the road to popular Maroon Lake and No's. 37 through 40 are reached along the Ashcroft Road. Four of these trips (No's. 32, 33, 34 and 37) in addition to No's. 30 and 31, whose trailheads are reached through Snowmass or Snowmass at Aspen, visit the Maroon Bells-Snowmass Wilderness. Spectacular Independence Pass and the slopes just to the west are traversed by No's. 41 through 45 and the last five trips (No's. 46 through 50) begin from Lincoln Creek Road that leaves Colorado 82 midway between Aspen and Independence Pass.

HOW TO USE THIS BOOK

Preceding the body of the text for each trail is an information capsule listing seven important facts:

3

Hikes are recommended as **one day trip** or **backpack.** A one day trip usually is short or lacks suitable sites for camping. A trip classified as a one day trip or a backpack (for which you carry overnight camping equipment) means the hike can be done in one day but because of the length, scenic attractions, possible side and loop trips or the availability of good campsites, you may prefer to take two or more days. A backpack only normally is too long or strenuous for the average hiker to make without a layover before returning.

Hiking **distance** is measured one way only.

Since many hikes have a loss of altitude that is subsequently regained, **elevation gain** is listed as the total footage increment, not just the difference between the highest and lowest points. Significant elevation loss, if any, also is shown.

Since you may need to allow extra time to make a trip that travels at an elevation substantially higher than that to which you are acclimated, the **high point** for each hike is given.

The **hiking time** is determined from a basic rate of two miles per hour plus allowances for rest stops, the steepness of the grade and the elevation gain. Trails are not graded according to difficulty, since this would necessitate a subjective evaluation that might not fit each individual's concept of an easy or hard hike. After a few trips you will be able to grade the trails for yourself by comparing the mileage and elevation gain, the major factors in determining how strenuous a hike will be, and by considering conditions such as the weather and how you feel on a specific day. Also, after a few hikes you will be able to predict whether your hiking speed generally is faster or slower than the times listed.

The **period when the trails are open** will vary each year depending upon the depth of the snow pack and the prevailing temperature. If you have doubts about a particular area, check with the district ranger station in Minturn, Carbondale, Eagle or Aspen, depending on which is closest to the trailhead, or contact the White River National Forest headquarters in Glenwood Springs.

The **U.S.G.S. topographic map(s) name, scale and date** are included because many of the side and loop trips suggested in the text are beyond the boundaries of the maps printed for each trail and you may want to purchase appropriate ones for the area not shown. In major cities U.S.G.S. topographic maps are sold through selected retail outlets or you can obtain them from the U.S. Government by sending $.75 and identifying information for each map to: Central Region-Map Distribution, U.S. Geological Survey, Denver Federal Center, Bldg. 41, Denver, Colorado 80225.

The text for each trail is in three main sections: the first section describes special features of the hike such as good viewpoints, impressive wild flower displays and possible side or loop trips. The second part gives driving directions. Although many of the access roads to the trailheads are unpaved, these generally have good surfaces. Sections of road that are steep, narrow or rough are noted. The remainder of the text describes the trail route and includes comments on points of interest along the way and directions for any side or loop trips. Extreme steepness, lack of water, unmarked junctions, difficult fords and other problems you may encounter are noted. Where appropriate, the numbers of other trails in this guide are given in the text, such as some references to side or loop trips.

The maps for each trail are enlarged or reduced sections of topographic maps produced by the U.S. Geological Survey. The items in red are those that are particularly important in helping you find, stay on and enjoy the trail. A legend for these items can be found following the Table of Contents. The trail mileages shown may not always agree with those on trail signs. Map mileages are taken from known points or have been interpolated from specific fixes. Frequently, you will see trails on the topographic maps that are not overlayed in red. They either have no relevance to the trail being described or are no longer maintained. Campsites are marked with open triangles and may or may not be improved. Campgrounds reached by roads are marked with a solid triangle. Water is not necessarily available at the identified campsites, although mention usually is made

4

in the text if the spot is "dry." Important sources of water not obvious from the topographic map are identified.

Topographic maps are simple in theory and enable you to visualize the terrain covered by a trail. Through interpretation of these maps you can determine to some extent beforehand the difficulty of the trail and the feasibility of making a loop or reaching a point off the main route. Also, in case you become confused, an ability to read a topographic map may make it easier for you to orient yourself.

The curvy lines on the topographic map are called contour lines and they connect points of equal elevation. The space between any two contour lines is termed a contour interval (in this book 40 feet) and is a measure of vertical distance. The closer the contour lines the steeper the terrain.

Unshaded areas on the topographic maps are regions of little or no vegetation. Original maps have a green overprint depicting areas with plant cover. In this book these appear as a medium to dark grey depending on the density of the green ink used in the original map. Figures along the contour lines, at the summits of peaks or elsewhere mark elevation above mean sea level. All maps in the book are north oriented.

Recreation maps prepared by the Forest Service are another good source of information, particularly for extended excursions. Although these maps show most of the latest trails and are an aid in planning side and loop trips, they do not show contour lines. Maps are available from the district ranger stations or the White River National Forest headquarters, Federal Building, Ninth and Grand Avenue, Glenwood Springs, Colorado 81601. All the trails described in this guide are within the boundaries of the White River National Forest. For a last minute source of information talk with ranger station personnel who have jurisdiction over the area you will be visiting. They often can tell you about new trail construction, road conditions and offer other helpful suggestions.

HIKING and BACKPACKING IN WEST CENTRAL COLORADO

Hiking and backpacking techniques are not discussed here because many fine books are available that cover the subject thoroughly. However, a few points concerning outdoor travel in the Colorado Rockies might be helpful:

Although many of the 50 trails described in this guide can be walked in tennis shoes, hiking boots with lug soles will give you better traction and more foot support. (Tennis shoes are good to have along to change into for fording streams and for camp wear.) Since you will be hiking frequently at high elevations across open terrain, you probably will want to wear sunglasses and if you sunburn easily a wide-brimmed hat and long-sleeved shirt are recommended.

Severe mountain storms can occur at anytime but after the first of September their likelihood increases with each successive day. For both comfort and safety always include a wool hat, gloves, a sweater, a windbreaker and a poncho or some other waterproof garment in your pack. A flashlight, iodine or some type of water purifying tablets and a first aid kit also should be standard equipment. Although mention is made in the text if water is not available along the trail, it is a good idea to begin each hike with a fresh bottle of drinking water.

Thunderstorms are a common weather phenomenon in the Colorado Rockies. Although lightning strikes are not confined to high, exposed places, you will be considerably safer on lower, wooded slopes. On hikes along open ridges or to a summit TURN AROUND AND RETREAT IF A THUNDERSTORM IS FORMING. These storms build very quickly but after a rapid progression of wind, hail or rain and lightning blue skies generally return quickly. Thunderstorms usually form in the early afternoon so you will have a better chance to make a dry hike if you start early.

Another, but less serious, problem is the mosquitoes you may encounter early in the season. An effective method of discouraging their attack is to use a spray repellent on clothes and a cream for exposed skin.

Most of the hikes begin at 9,000 feet or higher and many go over 12,000 feet so if you are accustomed to functioning at considerably lower elevations you will need several days to acclimatize to these heights. While hiking, a slow, steady pace is much more effective than short bursts of speed interrupted by long periods of rest.

Stream flow often is heavy at the beginning of the season. Fortunately, the volume of most streams varies drastically from early to late summer and what was a rushing torrent the end of June may present no problems by the end of July. Mention is made in the text of any fords that may be difficult.

Be sure to sign in at the registers placed near the start of some of the trails. Knowing how many people use the back country and where they go helps Forest Service personnel determine the best management of the area.

The authors recently hiked each of the trails in this book to insure that the most accurate and up-to-date information was available. However, trails change or are changed, either because of rock fall, washouts and other natural causes, or because the officials who maintain the trails decide to establish alternate routes. It is the intention of the authors to revise this volume every five years. If you wish to assist in this updating process, you're invited to send changes or irregularities noted on your hikes to the authors in care of The Touchstone Press, P.O. Box 81, Beaverton, Oregon 97005.

By enjoying the many delights offered by hiking and backpacking you accept an obligation both to the wilderness you are visiting and to those who will follow. Therefore, your presence should leave the wilderness unchanged. By adhering to this ethic you will cause the least damage to the environment and the least offense to your fellow outdoorsmen.

Leave no litter (including lunch refuse) and *take* no wild flowers, plant life or other specimens. Also, do not disturb the animals you may be fortunate enough to see. Aural blight can be as disturbing to others as the visual variety: for instance, loud shouting, radios or noisy dogs can be very annoying to those who are trying to enjoy wild sounds. Because their impact is greater, backpackers especially need to familiarize themselves with the proper techniques of locating and establishing campsites and the disposal of wastes.

Good hiking!

D. L.
R. L.

Contents

LEGEND

⬣	Starting Point
- - - -	Trail
········	Obscure Trail
△	Campsite
▲	Campground
■◣	Building or Remains
7.0	Mileage
No 51	Trail No.
125	Road No.
⌐≈⌐	Bridge
= = =	Secondary Road
▬▬▬	Primary Road

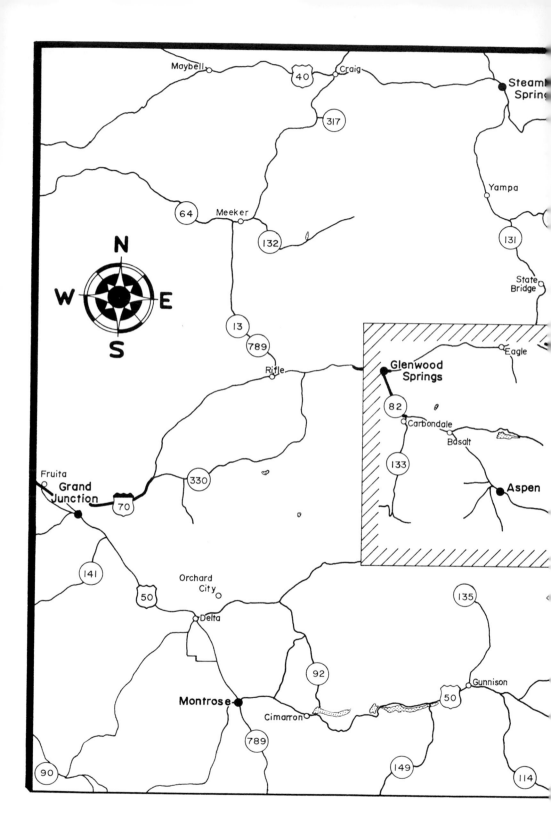

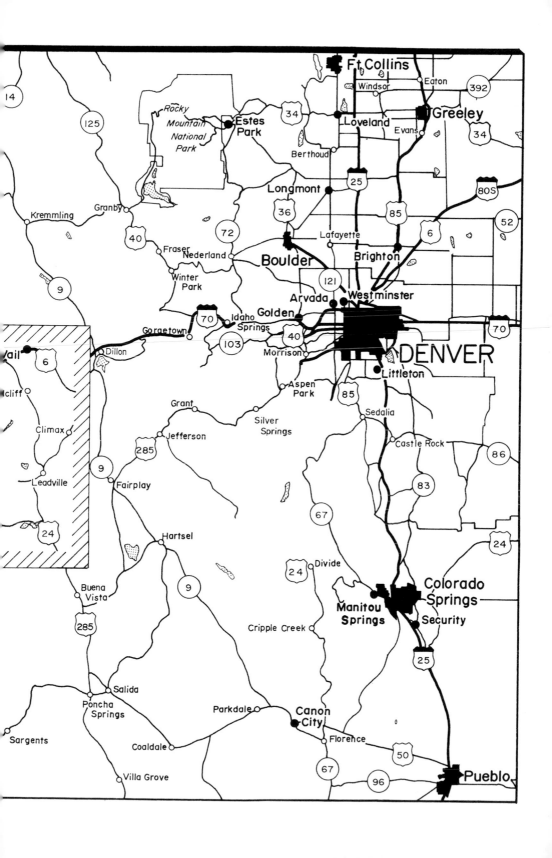

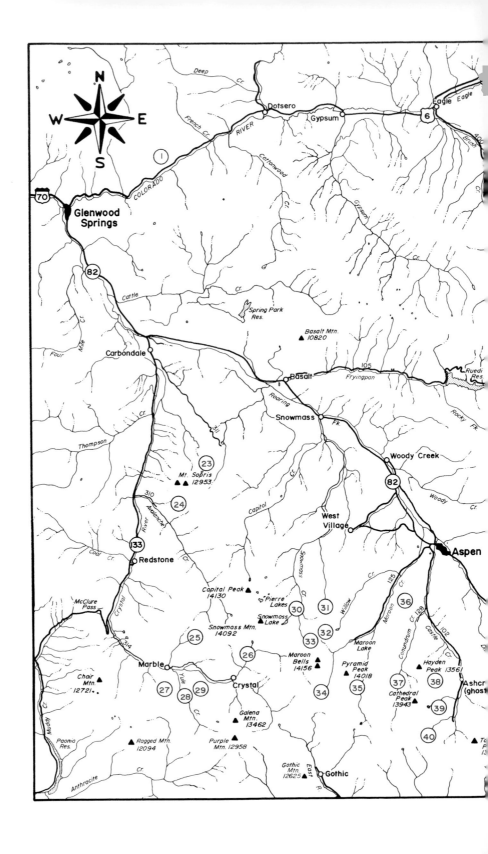

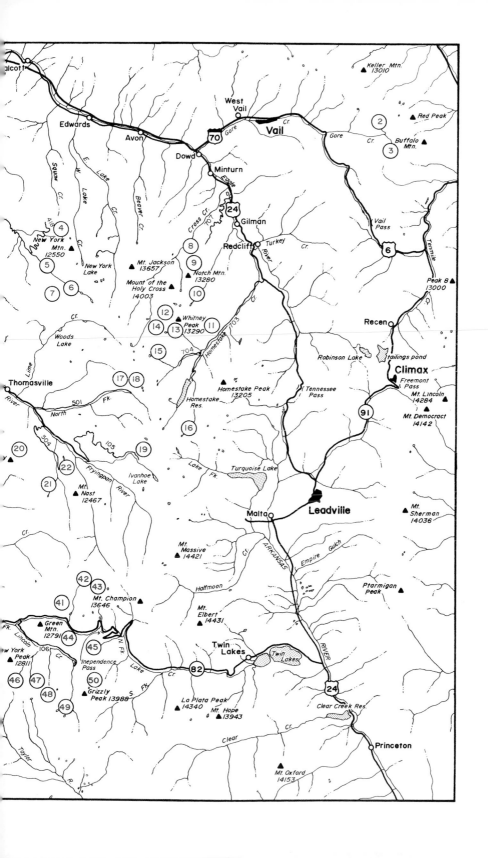

1 HANGING LAKE

One-half day trip
Distance: 1.6 miles one way
Elevation gain: 1,100 feet
High point: 7,200 feet
Allow 1 hour one way
Usually open April through October
Topographic map:
U.S.G.S. Shoshone, Colo.
7.5′   1961

You probably will spend almost as much time along the shore of Hanging Lake and at Bridal Veil Falls just above it as you did reaching these scenic, interesting landmarks. Most of the hike is along the narrow, wooded floor of Deadhorse Creek canyon. Its high steep walls, many rock outcroppings and the burbling creek provide an attractive setting. Carry water as the sources may be contaminated.

Proceed on U.S. 6-24 (Interstate 70) nine miles east of Glenwood Springs to a cluster of buildings on your left (north) and a sign stating Trail to Hanging Lake. Parking spaces are at the trailhead and across the highway. A picnic area and restrooms are located near the beginning of the hike.

Climb along a rocky, mostly treeless slope for 0.2 mile then make two very short switchbacks and cross a bridge over an underground creek. Recross the same stream bed on a second bridge after 0.1 mile and continue climbing. Keep left at a huge wooden sign identifying the side trail to Coffee Pot Springs. Hike uphill at a steady, moderate grade. As you walk farther into the canyon the trail surface becomes smoother and Deadhorse Creek begins flowing above ground.

Cross a third bridge at 0.5 mile, switchback and 0.1 mile farther cross another span. Continue up beside the stream. Come to the fifth bridge at 0.8 mile, make one set of switchbacks and traverse to the final span where a sign identifies a side path north to a toilet. At the west end of the bridge walk a few hundred feet at a gradual grade and pass a small shelter on your left then climb gradually by some especially interesting rock outcroppings. Squirrels are plentiful along this section of the trip. Travel through a more arid section of the canyon for a short distance before switchbacking right and traversing the wall above the floor. Wind up steep stone steps and come to a fork. Keep right and travel across a boardwalk to the shore of the lake.

To reach Bridal Veil Falls turn left at the fork just before the lake and go 100 yards, climbing very slightly, to the base of the cascade. The lower portion of the wall behind the falls has been eroded by water action so you can walk behind the torrent.

Falls above Hanging Lake

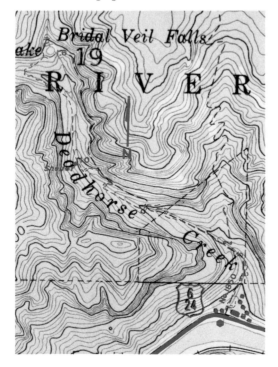

2 GORE LAKE

One day trip or backpack
Distance: 7 miles one way
Elevation gain: 2,660 feet
High point: 11,360 feet
Allow 3½ to 4 hours one way
Usually open July through September
Topographic maps:
  U.S.G.S. Vail East, Colo.
  7.5′   1970
  U.S.G.S. Willow Lakes, Colo.
  7.5′   1970

The narrow Gore Range extends south from near Green Mountain Reservoir to Climax and two hikes in this guide traverse the western slope of the central portion. The climb to Red Buffalo Pass (No. 3) ends at the crest of the range where you can look down to the eastern boundary of the chain. In contrast to the jagged peaks that surround Gore Lake, the slopes at the pass are open and grassy. The trailhead for both trips is only six miles from Vail and each makes either a good one day trip or backpack. Since the first five miles are the same you may want to visit both destinations if you are staying overnight.

The trail to Gore Lake climbs along the wall of the broad valley holding Gore Creek for five miles then turns sharply north and rises steeply one mile before winding through several lush basins. If you are backpacking, Snow Lake, one mile north of Gore Lake, is a good destination for a cross-country side trip.

Drive on U.S. 6 six miles east of Vail to a sign on the east side of the highway listing mileages to the Wilderness boundary, Main Gore Lake and other destinations. Parking spaces are available for several cars in front of the sign. The trailhead is 50 yards north of the entrance to Gore Creek Campground.

Climb erratically along the valley wall of grass and aspen, periodically rising steeply for short distances. Drop slightly and travel at a more moderate grade, crossing a few small side streams. Come close to Gore Creek before resuming the irregular climb. Travel through a zone of evergreens then near 2.0 miles drop slightly and walk beside a fork of Deluge Creek for several yards before coming to the crossing of the main flow in a shaded glen. This and the junction at 5.0 miles are good spots to rest.

Climb through woods, traverse briefly along an open slope and continue uphill through a forest of lodgepole pine. Near 2.3 miles pass a few small, stagnant ponds beside the trail. Begin walking at a more gradual grade and farther on traverse a treeless portion of the valley wall. Reenter woods at 4.0 miles and continue for one mile to the junction of the trail to Red Buffalo Pass.

Turn left (north), pass a grave site and begin winding steeply uphill near a rambunctious stream. After three-quarters mile cross a small creek and soon travel across several lush meadows. Resume climbing and wind up beneath large, more widely spaced trees to the edge of a bench a few hundred feet east of the lake. Although called Main Gore Lake, there are no lesser tarns nearby as the name implies.

14

Gore Creek Valley

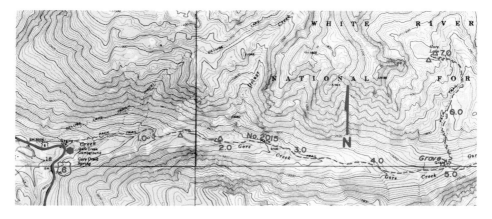

3 RED BUFFALO PASS

One day trip or backpack
Distance: 8 miles one way
Elevation gain: 3,000 feet
High point: 11,700 feet
Allow 4 to 5 hours one way
Usually open July through September
Topographic maps:
    U.S.G.S. Vail East, Colo.
    7.5′   1970
    U.S.G.S. Vail Pass, Colo.
    7.5′   1970
    U.S.G.S. Willow Lakes, Colo.
    7.5′   1970

From the grassy slopes of Red Buffalo Pass you can see the eastern edge of the narrow Gore Range and look west back down the broad valley you followed for the first two-thirds of the hike. A cluster of unnamed lakes lies 300 feet below the pass on the eastern slope and are a good destination for a short side trip. You can extend the hike even farther by continuing south from the tarns for 1.5 miles to Gore (Eccles) Pass. For the more adventurous, several peak climbs can be made from the vicinity of the Pass.

Proceed on U.S. 6 six miles east of Vail to a sign on the east side of the highway listing mileages to the Wilderness boundary, Main Gore Lake and other destinations. Parking for several cars is available in front of the sign. The trailhead is 50 yards north of the entrance to Gore Creek Campground.

Traverse the valley wall of grass and aspen, periodically climbing steeply. Drop slightly and travel at a more moderate grade, crossing a few shallow side streams. Come close to Gore Creek before resuming the irregular climb. Travel through a zone of evergreens then near 2.0 miles drop slightly and walk beside a fork of Deluge Creek for several yards before coming to the crossing of the main flow in a shaded glen. This and the junction at 5.0 miles are good spots to rest.

Climb through woods and near 2.3 miles pass a few, small stagnant ponds beside the trail. Begin walking at a more gradual grade and farther on traverse a large, treeless section of the valley wall. Reenter woods at 4.0 miles and continue for one mile to the junction of the trail to Gore Lake (No. 2).

Turn right, as indicated by the sign pointing to Gore-Willow Creek Pass, and ford Gore Creek. A log about 20 yards downstream may make the crossing easier. Climb gradually through woods and two clearings then curve right and travel across a larger open area. Reenter woods and rise at a moderate grade near Gore Creek and at 6.4 miles come to a meadow at the edge of the basin. Carefully note where the tread stops so you will follow the same trail you took up on your return. Walk along the right (southwest) side of the meadow, resume traveling on a well-defined trail and reenter woods. Begin climbing more steeply in short, loose switchbacks to an easy ford of Gore Creek at 7.0 miles.

Climb a few yards, immediately pass a campsite on your left then keep slightly right and head northeast through a meadow toward a tall stake. Continue beyond the marker across the grass for several yards then climb for a short distance on an obvious trail. Curve left and head north along an open bench. Begin climbing steeply and two-thirds mile from the meadow make two short switchbacks and come to a grassy slope and a cairn.

Pass the remains of a cabin on your right and traverse to the southeast along the open swath. Where the trail becomes faint you can either follow the stakes or, if you want to go directly to Red Buffalo Pass, turn left at the first marker and climb cross-country, bearing slightly right, for about 150 yards. From the pass a trail goes down to the unnamed lakes. If you choose to follow the stakes, continue up along the grassy slope and come near the crest. Turn left and walk 200 yards to the pass or turn right and hike south along the crest or just below it on the west side to a good viewpoint.

Lake east of Red Buffalo Pass

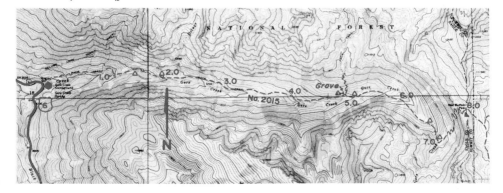

4 NOLAN LAKE

One day trip or backpack
Distance: 3.4 miles one way
Elevation gain: 1,500 feet; loss 160 feet
High point: 11,410 feet
Allow 2 hours one way
Usually open July through September
Topographic maps:
    U.S.G.S. Crooked Creek Pass, Colo.
    7.5'   1970
    U.S.G.S. Fulford, Colo.
    7.5'   1962

Four hikes described in this guide begin in the Fulford area southeast of Eagle. They range in difficulty from the 0.8 mile visit to the mouth of Fulford Cave (No. 5) to the considerably longer and more demanding trips to Mystic Island Lake (No. 6) and Charles Peak (No. 7).

Near the beginning of the climb to Nolan Lake the route winds through the ghost mining town of Fulford. Backpackers and hikers who want a strenuous side trip can head northeast from the junction at 2.7 miles toward New York Lake.

Drive on Interstate 70 east of Glenwood Springs or west of Vail to the Eagle exit. At that community turn south at the sign pointing to Sylvan Lake. Curve left after a few blocks then a few hundred feet farther come to a junction where a sign states Brush Creek and lists several mileages. Turn right and proceed 10 miles to a fork just before Brush Creek where the pavement ends. Keep left on County Road 415 then six miles farther keep straight (left) on the main road, following the sign to Yoeman Park. Continue 0.5 mile to a junction and turn left onto the road to Fulford and Triangle Creek. Travel uphill for three miles to the side road to the new settlement of Fulford. Keep straight (right) and after several yards pass the junction of a steep road on your right where a sign identifies the beginning of the Nolan Lake Trail. A small turnout is along the left (west) shoulder of the main road a short distance beyond the trailhead.

Climb east along the steep side road and after several hundred yards come to old Fulford. Near the center of the town keep right where the road forks and continue past some additional weathered structures. A few hundred yards beyond the site come to a sign indicating the route to Nolan Lake. Turn left and follow a road for about 0.5 mile to a huge log across the track. A few yards beyond it look for a sign pointing right to Nolan Lake.

Turn right onto a trail and hike at an irregular grade then climb steeply for a short distance. Resume following a more moderate grade and near 1.5 miles curve left into the valley holding Nolan Creek. Walk near the base of a massive scree slope then just beyond its end curve sharply left and scramble for several yards along the edge of a large boulder. Continue on a well-defined trail and soon begin climbing steeply. The waterfall on the south valley wall is the outlet from Nolan Lake. Near 2.6 miles level off and enter a grassy basin. Walk through the meadow toward a wooden sign facing the opposite direction. Hop a stream and come to the marker that gives mileages northeast to New York Lake and southwest to Nolan Lake.

Follow the metal tags to the south, cross two small streams and continue several yards over the grass to the resumption of the well-defined tread along a low bank on your right. Wind up through open woods for about 0.1 mile then pass a pond on your left and drop slightly through a little canyon formed by two rock outcroppings. Where the route becomes faint just beyond this small ravine, keep in the same direction you were heading and descend over slabs for several yards to the established trail. Continue downhill for the final few hundred yards to the inlet end of the lake.

Valley above Nolan Lake

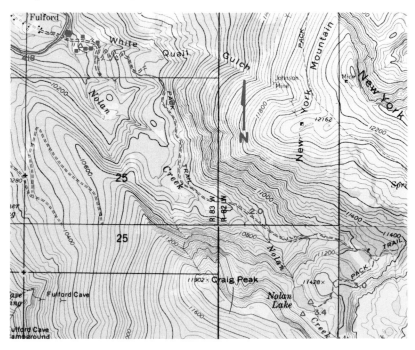

5 FULFORD CAVE

One-half day trip
Distance: 0.8 mile one way
Elevation gain: 560 feet
High point: 10,000 feet
Allow ½ hour one way
Usually open late June through September
Topographic map:
U.S.G.S. Crooked Creek Pass, Colo.
7.5′ **1970**

Although named for the nearby mining community of old Fulford, now a ghost town, the cave was discovered either in 1890 by a Captain Nolan Smith or two years later by a miner named Maxwell. Both men claimed credit but it was Maxwell who filed a mining claim and who, apparently, dug and timbered the entrance. Today the cave is popular with spelunkers. Carry water as the trail sources are not dependable.

Considerably longer hikes to Mystic Island Lake (No. 6) and Charles Peak (No. 7) begin near the trailhead to Fulford Cave and the first part of the trip to Nolan Lake (No. 4) winds past the remains of old Fulford.

Proceed on Interstate 70 east of Glenwood Springs or west of Vail to the Eagle exit. At that community turn south at the sign pointing to Sylvan Lake. Curve left after a few blocks then a few hundred feet farther come to a junction where a sign states Brush Creek and lists several mileages. Turn right and drive 10 miles to a fork just before Brush Creek where the pavement ends. Keep left on County Road 415 then six miles farther keep straight (left) on the main road, following the sign to Yoeman Park. Continue 0.5 mile to a junction and keep straight (right), as indicated by the sign pointing to Fulford Cave Campground, and go about 1.5 miles. Bear left at the entrance to the campground and after 200 feet come to a large parking area. A small sign on the left (north) bank before the turnouts states Fulford Cave ¾.

Climb for 100 feet and pass through a gate then wind uphill at a gradual grade through woods of aspen and grass. Be sure to stay on the new trail grade. Begin rising more steeply and near 0.4 mile travel up a ravine. Turn sharply right where a path goes left 40 feet to Fulford Cave Spring. Traverse an open slope and 200 feet from the path to the spring come to a stake at an unsigned junction. The path that continues straight ahead goes several feet to a small digging. Turn left and climb in a few short switchbacks to the entrance to the cave. Caution: do not enter the cave unless you are familiar with underground exploration techniques. The right (east) entrance has a dropoff a few feet from the opening.

Aspens from entrance to the cave

Cave entrance

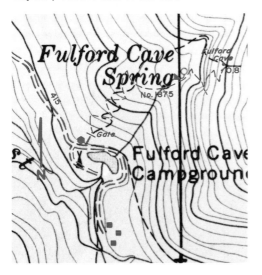

6 MYSTIC ISLAND LAKE

One day trip or backpack
Distance: 6 miles one way
Elevation gain: 1,850 feet
High point: 11,300 feet
Allow 3 to 3½ hours one way
Usually open July through September
Topographic maps:
  U.S.G.S. Crooked Creek Pass, Colo.
  7.5'   1970
  U.S.G.S. Mt. Jackson, Colo.
  7.5'   1970

Most moderately long trails that gain elevation pass through zones of differing vegetation and the climb along the large, convoluted valley of East Brush Creek to Mystic Island Lake is no exception. The hike travels through aspen then conifers and several meadows before reaching timberline at the head of the valley. Most of the grade is gradual to moderate and those desiring a shorter hike might wish to stop at the alpine setting of Lake Charles at 4.6 miles. Although camp sites are available at Mystic Island Lake the area around Lake Charles offers more satisfactory choices.

Two other hikes begin near the trailhead: a short, easy trip to the mouth of Fulford Cave (No. 5) and a 4.9 mile long route climbs to Charles Peak (No. 7), high on the rim of the valley you traverse to reach Mystic Island Lake.

Drive on Interstate 70 east of Glenwood Springs or west of Vail to the Eagle exit. At that community turn south at the sign pointing to Sylvan Lake. Curve left after a few blocks then a few hundred feet farther come to a junction where a sign states Brush Creek and lists several mileages. Turn right and proceed 10 miles to a fork just before Brush Creek where the pavement ends. Keep left on County Road 415 then six miles farther keep straight (left) on the main road, following the sign to Yoeman Park. Continue 0.5 mile to a junction and keep straight (right), as indicated by the sign pointing to Fulford Cave Campground, and go about 1.5 miles. Bear left at the entrance to the campground and after 200 feet come to a large parking area.

Walk east from the parking turnouts along the road for 150 yards to a fork. Keep left, following the sign stating East Brush Creek and indicating the direction to Lake Charles. Climb moderately along the slope and soon begin traveling through an attractive aspen woods. Near 0.3 mile conifers begin replacing the aspen and the roadbed narrows into a trail. Continue uphill at an erratic, but always easy, grade. At 1.0 mile travel away from the stream then return to it after 0.2 mile. Walk very close to the bank and look for the resumption of the main trail across the flow. Go upstream another few yards to a wide foot log and make the crossing.

Climb through woods for 1.5 miles to a wide log bridge at a second crossing. Travel rather steeply uphill for one-third mile then level off and pass through a meadow with a pond. Resume winding up through woods for 0.1 mile and come to a smaller meadow. Make two easy stream crossings then descend slightly before climbing through an area of rock slabs and conifers. Near 4.6 miles where you see a bridge to your right walk to it for a view of the outlet end of Lake Charles.

To complete the hike to Mystic Island Lake return to the main trail. Traverse the slope above the north side of Lake Charles then drop to near the shore for a few yards to its eastern end. Climb through an area of grass and rocks for one-quarter mile to the edge of a long, marshy meadow. Traverse along the slope at a level grade, looking ahead or downslope where the trail is faint. at the east end resume winding uphill for 0.1 mile to a wide stream. Turn left and parallel the flow then follow it as it curves right. Pass a tarn and come to the north end of Mystic Island Lake.

Brush Creek

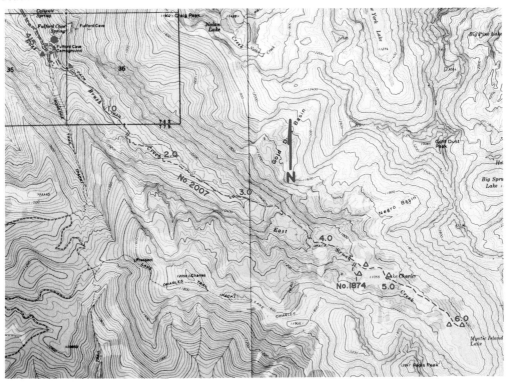

7 CHARLES PEAK

One day trip
Distance: 4.9 miles one way
Elevation gain: 2,350 feet
High point: 12,000 feet
Allow 3 to 3½ hours one way
Usually open late June through September
Topographic map:
U.S.G.S. Crooked Creek Pass, Colo.
7.5′   **1970**

The complex, circuitous route to Charles Peak travels through woods, a logged area and across grassy slopes above timberline to the crest of the southern wall of rugged East Brush Creek valley. Those wanting a more strenuous trip can continue along the main trail beyond the turnoff to Charles Peak and climb Fools Peak. Two other hikes, No's. 5 and 6, begin near the trailhead.

Proceed on Interstate 70 east of Glenwood Springs or west of Vail to the Eagle exit. At that community turn south at the sign pointing to Sylvan Lake. Curve left after a few blocks then a few hundred feet farther come to a junction where a sign states Brush Creek and lists several mileages. Turn right and drive 10 miles to a fork just before Brush Creek where the pavement ends. Keep left on County Road 415 then six miles farther keep straight (left) on the main road, following the sign to Yoeman Park. Continue 0.5 mile to a junction and keep straight (right) as indicated by the sign pointing to Fulford Cave Campground, and go about 1.5 miles. Bear left at the entrance to the campground and after 200 feet come to a large parking area.

Walk east from the parking turnouts along the road for 150 yards to a fork and follow the lower (right) road for 0.1 mile to a gate. Veer right onto a path, identified by

a sign pointing to Iron Edge Trail. Descend slightly and cross two footbridges then travel along a slope of grass and brush on a sometimes faint trail. Occasionally, the vegetation is dense but you easily can push through it. About 0.1 mile from the bridges hop a small creek then several yards farther come to a second stream. After crossing it curve right and look ahead several yards for the resumption of the obvious trail. Traverse an open, grassy slope for a short distance then enter woods and come to an unsigned junction.

Switchback left and recross the grassy slope. Enter deeper woods and cross a small side stream. Switchback a few times before winding up through the forest at a moderate grade. At 1.1 miles come to a flat area and travel on the level beside a small stream. Ford the flow at a broad, shallow place, curve right and resume climbing.

At 2.0 miles come to the edge of a logged area. Carefully note landmarks along the route for the next 1.5 miles so you will have no problems locating the correct route on your return. Bear left and climb along a cat road for about 100 feet to a crossroad. Turn right and after 200 feet turn left at another road. Climb in several switchbacks, turning left after the first one where a spur road goes right, for 0.5 mile to a broad saddle and the junction of a Forest Service road. Turn left and walk up the main road. Just beyond a sign indicating closure to 4-wheel drive vehicles come to a fork and keep right. One-tenth mile farther come to two rough spurs on your left. Take the right (middle) one and follow it up to the south for 0.1 mile to a wooded saddle and a cluster of signs.

Turn left, as indicated by an arrow pointing to Lake Charles, and walk through woods for a short distance to a grassy slope. Reenter woods and traverse at a generally moderate grade. Drop slightly and cross a small side stream, the last source of water. Continue traversing for a short distance to the remains of a cabin. The trail curves left and climbs for 100 yards to timberline. Note where the trail leaves the woods.

Climb along the open slope, bearing slightly right, and after a few hundred feet resume traveling on an obvious tread. As the trail begins traversing the south slope, turn left and climb cross-country for about 75 yards to the crest.

Eagle Peak from Charles Peak

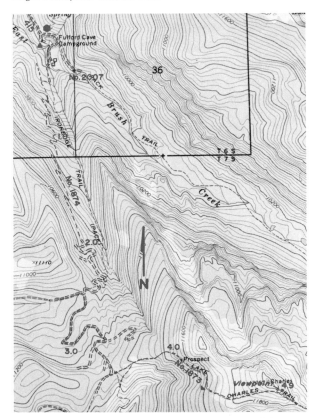

8 HALF MOON PASS

One day trip
Distance: 3 miles one way
Elevation gain: 1,750 feet
High point: 11,900 feet
Allow 2 to 2½ hours one way
Usually open July through September
Topographic map:
 U.S.G.S. Mount of the Holy Cross, Colo.
 7.5'   1970

Three trails begin from Half Moon Campground, located southwest of Vail. Two of the trips climb to views of the famous configuration on the east face of Mount of the Holy Cross: the route to a high point on the southern flank of Notch Mountain (No. 9) follows a well-graded trail to the superb and much-photographed sighting of the cross and the second climbs to Half Moon Pass then traverses cross-country to a view from a more northerly angle. The third hike, to Lake Constantine (No. 10), follows the same route as the one to Notch Mountain for the first two miles then continues traversing the high, wooded valley wall to the head of the basin.

The one mile of cross-country travel from Half Moon Pass along the northwest slope of Notch Mountain is not difficult and involves only 300 feet of elevation gain. In addition to seeing the Mount of the Holy Cross from the viewpoint you can see down to Lake Patricia on the floor of the rugged, narrow canyon squeezed between the slopes of the Mount and Notch Mountain. However, if you want a shorter hike, Half Moon Pass, with views of the Gore and Mosquito Ranges to the east and the Cross Creek Basin to the west, is a good place to end the trip. Carry water as none is available along the route.

Drive on U.S. 24 two miles south of Minturn or 19 miles north of Tennessee Pass to a sign pointing west to Half Moon Campground. Turn west and proceed eight miles along a sometimes rough and moderately steep, but passable, dirt road to its end at a large turnout just beyond the entrance to Half Moon Campground. A sign on the west side of turnaround stating Half Moon Trail marks the beginning of the hike.

Wind up along the slope of grass and trees at a moderately steep grade. Near 1.2 miles the timber becomes sparse and scattered. Hike up through the open area, switchbacking a few times, to a sign identifying Half Moon Pass. Continue along the main trail, descending into a grove of conifers, then traverse a talus slope. About one-third mile from the Pass, just beyond the rocky area and about 200 yards from the end of the woods, look for five snags on your right and three on the left.

Turn left, leaving the established route that continues downhill to East Cross Creek, and climb along the grassy slope. Go uphill just high enough to keep above timberline. Mount of the Holy Cross comes into view soon after you begin traveling cross-country. Eventually, you will see a large outcropping ahead on the slope you are traversing. Go just above or below it and continue at about the same elevation for approximately one-third mile to the viewpoint at a cluster of boulders. You will cross a few small rocky areas near the end of the cross-country traverse but the going should present no problems. However, travel beyond the rocky viewpoint is difficult.

26

Mount of the Holy Cross from the north

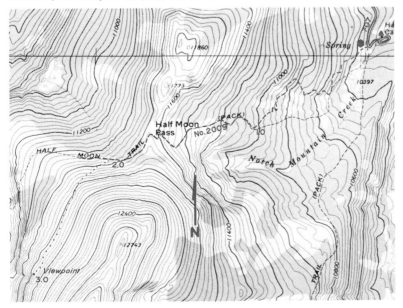

9 NOTCH MOUNTAIN

One day trip or backpack
Distance: 5 miles one way
Elevation gain: 2,930 feet
High point: 13,100 feet
Allow 3 to 3½ hours one way
Usually open July through September
Topographic map:
    U.S.G.S. Mount of the Holy Cross, Colo.
    7.5'   **1970**

Winding up the well-graded trail to the large stone shelter cabin on the south shoulder of Notch Mountain is, in itself, an enjoyable climb. But even if the ascent were not so scenic the trip still would be exceptional because of the view at the end. Slightly more than one mile away looms the east face of Mount of the Holy Cross with its famous configuration.

Even before the 1800's trappers and others frequenting the rugged area had told of a giant cross of snow on the face of a high peak but the first printed account did not appear until 1869. The first photograph was taken four years later and the phenomenon became well known. From the late twenties through the late thirties pilgrimages to the summit of Notch Mountain were frequent and a few groups made the considerably more rugged trip to the Bowl of Tears, a lake on the valley floor between Mount of the Holy Cross and Notch Mountain. The Mount was a National Monument from 1929 to 1950 when it was withdrawn because of the declining number of tourists and the difficulty of maintaining access to the viewpoint. During the years between 1938 and 1950 the area was part of the Camp Hale Army Reservation where U.S. ski troopers trained in World War II.

Drive on U.S. 24 two miles south of Minturn or 19 miles north of Tennessee Pass to a sign pointing west to Half Moon Campground. Turn west and proceed eight miles along a sometimes rough and moderately steep, but passable, dirt road to its end at a large turnout just beyond the entrance to Half Moon Campground. A sign on the east side of the parking area identifies the beginning of the trail to Lake Constantine (No. 10) and Notch Mountain.

Climb through woods, passing a few grassy areas, at an irregular but never steep grade. For the first 0.8 mile the trail travels up the face of a broad slope then the route begins traversing the steep valley wall. Drop slightly, resume climbing and cross a slide area. Reenter deep woods and soon cross a small side stream, the only source of water along the hike. Traverse at a gradual grade and pass the edge of a scree patch. Drop, then climb more noticeably and wind up to the junction of the trail to Lake Constantine.

Turn right and traverse the slope of grass and scattered trees. Make a few sets of short switchbacks and resume traversing the slope of grass and a few bushes and trees where marmots are plentiful. Climb in switchbacks along the east side of a ridge. You can look northeast to the mining town of Gilman clinging to the steep slope of the Eagle Valley about four miles away. At 3.0 miles make the first of the approximately two dozen switchbacks to the summit. Their length becomes increasingly short as they near the top but the grade always is steady and moderate. As you gain elevation you will have views east to the Gore and Mosquito Ranges and, considerably closer, onto three large tarns on benches below to the south. Also, Lake Constantine is visible for a brief time. Whitney Peak is the mountain forming the southeastern wall of the valley below. Make the final switchback to the left near the crest and traverse gradually uphill over the rocky tundra to the stone cabin. The actual summit of Notch Mountain is 0.5 mile to the north and 240 feet higher. A more northerly view of Mount of the Holy Cross can be seen from the trail over Half Moon Pass (No. 8).

Mount of the Holy Cross from shelter cabin

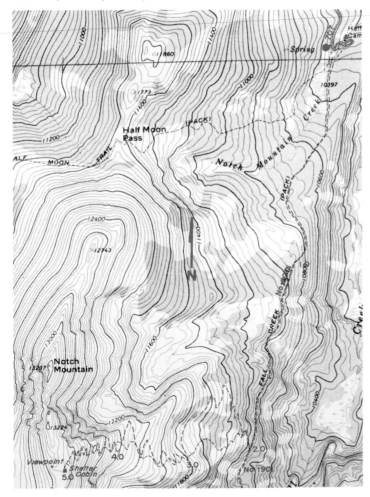

10 LAKE CONSTANTINE

One day trip or backpack
Distance: 3.5 miles one way
Elevation gain: 1,340 feet; loss 220 feet
Hight point: 11,420 feet
Allow 2 hours one way
Usually open July through September
Topographic map:
   U.S.G.S. Mount of the Holy Cross, Colo.
   7.5'   **1970**

Lake Constantine lies between Notch Mountain and Whitney Peak near the head of the deep valley holding Fall Creek. The hike along the wooded wall to the meadow at the north end of the lake is a good choice for a one day trip or a backpack. Those wanting a longer journey can follow the path south from the lake for 1.5 miles, gaining 1,200 feet of elevation, to Fall Creek Pass then descend into the complex, rugged basin that holds Seven Sisters Lakes and myriads of tarns (No. 12). The junction of the route to Notch Mountain (No. 9) and the famous view of the crucifix on the east face of Mount of the Holy Cross is midway along the main trail to Lake Constantine. Another route to a sighting of the Mount begins opposite the trailhead (No. 8).

Drive on U.S. 24 two miles south of Minturn or 19 miles north of Tennessee Pass to a sign pointing west to Half Moon Campground. Turn west and proceed eight miles along a sometimes rough and moderately steep, but passable, dirt road to its end at a large turnout just beyond the entrance to Half Moon Campground. A sign on the east side of the parking area identifies the beginning of the trail to Lake Constantine and Notch Mountain.

Climb through woods, passing a few grassy areas, at an irregular but never steep grade. For the first 0.8 mile the trail travels up the face of a broad slope then the route begins traversing the steep valley wall. Drop slightly, resume climbing and cross a slide area. Reenter deep woods and soon cross a small side stream. Periodically, you will be able to look down to the large meadows on the valley floor and east to portions of U.S. 24. Traverse at a gradual grade and pass near the edge of a scree patch. Drop, then climb more noticeably and wind up to the junction of the trail to Notch Mountain at 2.0 miles.

Keep straight (left) and traverse the steep, sparsely wooded slope then drop slightly to a stream crossing and resume climbing. At 2.7 miles pass through a notch on the valley wall and enter deep woods. Descend then travel uphill at an irregular grade through more open terrain of brush, rocks, grass and scattered trees. Along this stretch you can examine the rugged southeastern side of Notch Mountain towering overhead. Drop slightly, cross a footbridge and resume hiking uphill then walk gradually downhill through a meadow for several hundred yards to the northwestern tip of Lake Constantine. This final portion of the trail through the grass is faint or nonexistent but the correct route is obvious. Whitney Peak is above the lake to the southeast.

Trail bridge

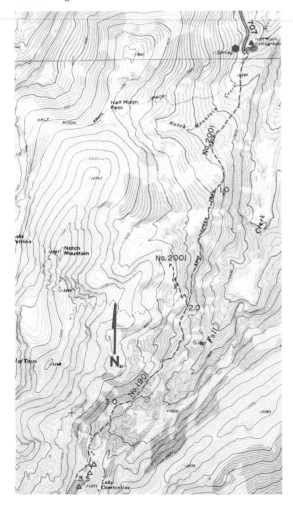

11 WHITNEY LAKE

One day trip or backpack
Distance: 3 miles one way
Elevation gain: 1,860 feet
High point: 10,960 feet
Allow 2 hours one way
Usually open late June through September
Topographic map:
U.S.G.S. Mount of the Holy Cross, Colo.
7.5′   1970

In the early 1880's much mining activity occurred north of Tennessee Pass, including the Homestake Creek area southwest of Vail. However, the Homestake boom was short-lived and by 1884 the two largest towns, Gold Park and Holy Cross City, were almost deserted. Today, recreationists and personnel maintaining the water diversion projects drive over the roads once taken by stagecoaches and wagons and only the remains of Holy Cross City and scattered, obscure foundations are evidence of the frenetic activity that occurred almost a century ago.

Six trails described in this guide probe the slopes of the Homestake area. All the trips are suitable for both one day outings or backpacks. The hikes to the rugged basin holding the Seven Sisters Lakes (No. 12) and the remains of Holy Cross City (No. 13) follow the same route for the first 3.3 miles and the treks to Fancy Lake (No. 14) and

Missouri Lakes (No. 15) can be combined into an extremely scenic loop. All the trails climb the west slope of the Homestake area except for the hike along the East Fork of Homestake Creek to Lonesome Lake (No. 16) at the extreme southern end of the drainage.

The climb to tree-rimmed Whitney Lake is a good choice for a first hike in the Homestake area. Except for the initial 0.5 mile the grade is moderate as the trail rises through two grassy meadows and woods of aspen and spruce.

Drive on U.S. 24 10 miles south of Minturn or 11 miles north of Tennessee Pass to a sign stating Blodgett Campground, Gold Park and Trails to High Lakes. Turn southwest and travel on the unpaved road four miles to a sign on your right reading Whitney Lake 3. Space for parking your car is on the left side of the road across from the trailhead.

Climb steeply along an old road that has been closed to vehicular traffic. Come to an overlook then continue through aspen at a more moderate grade. At 0.5 mile traverse gradually along the lower edge of a grassy area. Near its southwestern corner curve right and climb to the woods at the top of the meadow where the road ends.

Traverse to the west along a well-defined trail and near one mile make a loose set of switchbacks. After a short distance come to a second grassy area. Just as you leave the woods you can look southwest up the valley to Homestake Dam. Near the top of the meadow pass an unsigned cross trail that heads southwest to the Holy Cross City road. Reenter aspen woods and continue climbing.

At 1.9 miles turn right into the side canyon formed by Whitney Creek. The vegetation changes abruptly from the deciduous aspen to conifers. After 200 yards cross Whitney Creek then walk along the west side of the canyon for a few hundred feet before curving right and traversing the face of the slope. The grade increases slightly and winds through the forest then becomes gradual until the final short climb to the southeastern end of the lake. Whitney Peak rises prominently to the northwest. The southwestern and northern sides of the mountain can be studied during the hikes to Seven Sisters Lakes and Lake Constantine (No. 10).

Whitney Lake

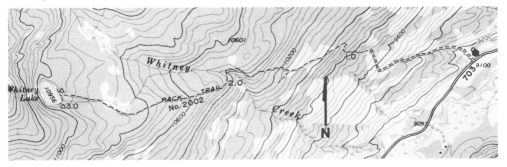

12 SEVEN SISTERS LAKES

One day trip or backpack
Distance: 5.6 miles one way
Elevation gain: 3,300 feet
High point: 12,600 feet
Allow 3 to 3½ hours one way
Usually open July through September
Topographic map:
    U.S.G.S. Mount of the Holy Cross, Colo.
    7.5′   **1970**

Although you can visit the lower portion of the massive and grandly scenic basin that holds the Seven Sisters Lakes and take a short side trip to the many remains of Holy Cross City (No. 13) in one day, this hike is an excellent choice for a backpack. In addition to a more thorough exploration of the

basin and the terrain surrounding the old mining town, you could follow the trail over Fall Creek Pass to Lake Constantine (No. 10) or make a cross-country climb of Whitney Peak from the pass.

Drive on U.S. 24 10 miles south of Minturn or 11 miles north of Tennessee Pass to a sign stating Blodgett Campground, Gold Park and Trails to High Lakes. Turn southwest and travel on the unpaved, but smooth and mostly level, road for eight miles to a large turnout on the west side of the road where a sign lists mileages to Hunky Dory Lake and Holy Cross City.

The beginning of the hike is a public right of way through private property so be sure to stay on the official route. Climb along the rocky jeep road for 0.2 mile then curve right and traverse at a moderate grade. At 0.7 mile switchback left and continue traversing then begin climbing more steeply. Keep right where a side road joins on the left. Between 2.1 and 2.3 miles the grade becomes more moderate and early in the summer this section may be swampy. Resume climbing noticeably then at 2.7 miles come to the edge of a basin of grass and scattered brush and trees. Near 2.9 miles meet a fork where a sign points left to Holy Cross City. Turn left and after a short distance come to a second, but unsigned, fork. The road to the left climbs for one mile, gaining 250 feet, to the town site.

Keep right and climb moderately along the road for 0.4 mile to Hunky Dory Lake. The name is connected with a mine, the Hunkidori, that operated in the vicinity during the early 1880's. Hike just above the lake then drop slightly to near the northeastern shore and cross the outlet creek. A few hundred feet farther ford a second, shallow stream and pass a few pieces of rusted machinery and the remains of a cabin. Beyond the lake where the roadbed becomes faint veer slightly left onto a trail.

Climb moderately along the floor of the valley then at 4.0 miles curve right and wind up above timberline to a bench with a few ponds. The rocky slope towering above on your right is the southwestern side of Whitney Peak. Resume winding up and come to a bench with a large tarn. The trail continues up between the grass-covered outcroppings to the first of the Seven Sisters Lakes. Fall Creek Pass at 12,600 feet is 1.4 miles farther.

Valley below Seven Sisters Lakes

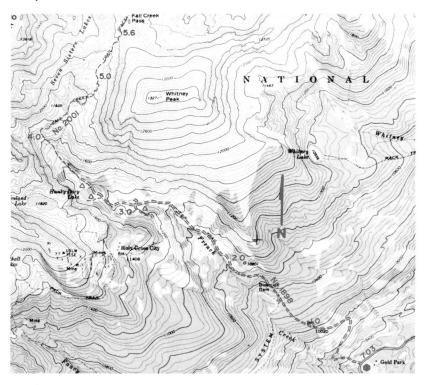

13 HOLY CROSS CITY

One day trip or backpack
Distance: 4 miles one way
Elevation gain: 2,200 feet
High point: 11,500 feet
Allow 2 to 2½ hours one way
Usually open July through September
Topographic map:
   U.S.G.S. Mount of the Holy Cross, Colo.
   7.5'   1970

In 1879 gold was discovered in the Eagle Valley north of Tennessee Pass. Some communities established after this date survived, such as Redcliff, Gilman and Minturn, but most flourished and then quickly died. Holy Cross City, above Gold Park, existed from 1880 to 1884 and at its peak supported a population of 300 people. A short boom in the late 1890's revived the town briefly. The name was derived from the Holy Cross Mining District—the famous mountain, although only 3.5 miles to the north, is not visible from the town site. Today, the relatively well-preserved remains of several buildings and some rusted machinery offer clues to the original character of the community.

In addition to being an interesting one day hike, the journey to Holy Cross City makes a good backpack as several side trips are possible. An especially scenic excursion

is to the massive basin holding the Seven Sisters Lakes (No. 12). From the meadow at Holy Cross City you can make shorter extensions by heading northwest for one mile to Cleveland Lake or visiting Mulhall Lakes and Fancy Lake and Pass (No. 14).

Proceed on U.S. 24 10 miles south of Minturn or 11 miles north of Tennessee Pass to a sign stating Blodgett Campground, Gold Park and Trails to High Lakes. Turn southwest and travel on the unpaved, but smooth and mostly level, road for eight miles to a large turnout on the west side of the road where a sign lists mileages to Hunky Dory Lake and Holy Cross City.

The beginning of the hike is a public right of way through private property so be sure to stay on the official route. Climb along the rocky jeep road for 0.2 mile then curve right and traverse at a moderate grade. At 0.7 mile switchback left and continue traversing then begin climbing steeply. During the short life of Holy Cross City a stage managed to negotiate this steep, rough road regularly. Keep right where a side road joins on the left. Between 2.1 and 2.3 miles the grade becomes more moderate and, in contrast to the rough surface along most of the route, this stretch sometimes is swampy and logs have been place across the bed. Resume climbing noticeably then at 2.7 miles come to the edge of a basin of grass and scattered brush and trees. Near 2.9 miles meet a fork where a sign points left to Holy Cross City. Turn left and after a short distance come to a second, but unsigned, fork. The road to the right passes Hunky Dory Lake and a trail continues to the Seven Sisters Lakes.

Keep left then curve left and climb for 0.1 mile to a bench where you will have views to the east and northeast. Continue along the road and at 3.8 miles pass below the remains of the stamp mill. Curve right and climb to a large, grassy basin and the remains of several buildings.

The road skirts the south edge of the lush valley and comes to a signed junction. The trail to the right goes to Cleveland Lake and the road continues south and west toward Mulhall Lakes and Fancy Lake and Pass. The trip to Cleveland Lake would add a total of two miles and 300 feet of elevation gain and the hike to Mulhall Lakes would involve two miles round trip and 400 feet of climbing. Fancy Lake is 1.5 miles from the junction and 200 feet higher.

Old cabin at Holy Cross City

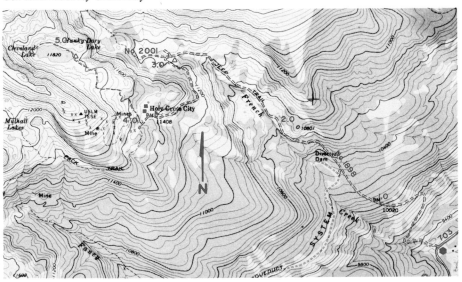

14 FANCY LAKE

One day trip or backpack
Distance: 2.3 miles one way (to Fancy Lake)
Elevation gain: 1,650 feet (to Fancy Lake)
High point: 11,540 feet (Fancy Lake)
Allow 1½ to 2 hours one way (to Fancy Lake)
Usually open July through September
Topographic maps:
    U.S.G.S. Mount Jackson, Colo.
    7.5'   1970
    U.S.G.S. Mount of the Holy Cross, Colo.
    7.5'   1970

The final 0.3 mile of the short, often steep, climb to Fancy Lake is cross-country and necessitates some route finding. Reaching the scenic, timberline setting of the circular lake, however, is just the first of the many possible and equally attractive destinations: you can head northeast to Mulhall Lakes or Holy Cross City (No. 13) or beyond to Cleveland Lake. The trip to the first involves 1.0 mile and 350 feet of uphill one way and the trek to the remains of the mining town is 1.5 miles with 200 feet of elevation gain. Fancy Pass, 0.9 mile from and 850 feet above Fancy Lake affords a view down onto Treasure Vault and Blodgett Lakes and a trail drops from the pass, losing 700 feet, to Treasure Vault Lake. A superb loop is possible by climbing south from here for 0.6 mile and 300 feet over Missouri Pass then winding down and returning to your starting point along the trail past Missouri Lakes (No. 15). The entire circuit would be 10.2 miles long and involve 2,450 feet of elevation gain.

Drive on U.S. 24 ten miles south of Minturn or 11 miles north of Tennessee Pass to a sign stating Blodgett Campground, Gold Park and Trails to High Lakes. Turn south-west and travel on the unpaved, but smooth and mostly level, road for 8.5 miles to a road on your right that may be marked by a sign pointing to Missouri Lakes. Turn right, drive uphill for 1.6 miles to a large turnout on your right just before a small sign identifying Fancy Creek and leave your car here. (If you are doing the Fancy-Missouri Lakes loop, you can continue 0.4 mile farther to a diversion pipe then walk up beside it until you intersect the route to Fancy Lake.)

Walk up the old roadbed that climbs steeply from the west side of the turnout for 150 yards to a road paralleling the water diversion pipe. Continue in the direction you were traveling and hike up the steep road to the diversion dam. Keep right and continue climbing on a road. The grade becomes more moderate as the route travels up the wooded slope. The route passes a side creek and farther on, near 1.5 miles, the road narrows into a trail. Continue up then travel near the rim of a narrow and deep rocky gorge.

Cross a creek and about 15 yards beyond it come to a grassy little meadow. Ford a second, slightly larger stream and cross the clearing to its upper end where the tread resumes. Travel uphill through woods for a few hundred feet to a more open area. Look slightly left for a path. Follow it up along the slope of grass and rocks for several hundred feet until the tread becomes too faint to follow. Curve right and climb cross-country in a northwesterly direction. If you look ahead frequently and choose suitable routes, you should encounter no problems. Continue climbing steeply, bearing slightly right, to above the outlet end of Fancy Lake.

To make any of the possible side trips cross the outlet creek and head east and north for 100 feet. Walk through a little canyon of rock outcroppings for 100 yards to a road. To reach Mulhall Lakes, Holy Cross City and Cleveland Lake turn right. If any of the other destinations are your goal turn left and climb steeply along the rocky road. Enter a rugged, massive rocky canyon and wind up through the rubble to Fancy Pass. From the junction above Treasure Vault Lake keep left and follow the trail south up to Missouri Pass. If you do the trip before August you probably will encounter snow on the east sides of Fancy and Missouri Passes.

Fancy Lake

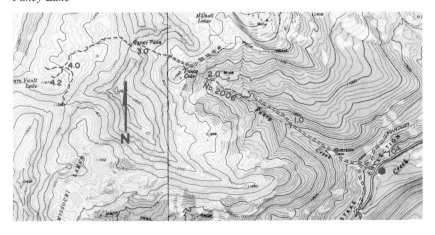

15 MISSOURI LAKES

One day trip or backpack
Distance: 3.9 miles one way
            (Upper Missouri Lake)
Elevation gain: 1,400 feet
            (Upper Missouri Lake)
High point: 11,550 feet (Upper Missouri Lake)
Allow 2 to 2½ hours one way
    (Upper Missouri Lake)
Usually open July through September
Topographic maps:
    U.S.G.S. Mount Jackson, Colo.
    7.5'   1970
    U.S.G.S. Mount of the Holy Cross, Colo.
    7.5'   1970

The trail to the Missouri Lakes is an excellent choice both for those who want a scenic, moderately easy trip in the Homestake area and for persons desiring a strenuous trek. The former group leisurely can explore the gentle, grassy, tree-dotted terrain around the lakes and the latter can continue up to Missouri Pass, an additional mile with 400 feet of elevation gain. An even longer hike is possible by descending from the Pass to Treasure Vault Lake, 300 feet below. You can combine the Missouri and Fancy Lakes trails into an exceptionally attractive loop. The complete circuit would involve 10.2 miles and 2,450 feet of elevation gain. (See No. 14 for details.)

Proceed on U.S. 24 ten miles south of Minturn or 11 miles north of Tennessee Pass to a sign stating Blodgett Campground, Gold Park and Trails to High Lakes. Turn southwest and travel on the unpaved, but smooth and mostly level, road for 8.5 miles to a road on your right that may be marked by a sign pointing to Missouri Lakes. Turn right

and drive uphill for two miles to a fork in the road at a huge water diversion pipe. (Those making the loop or who do not want to go the remaining distance can park here. Follow the shaded old road that is blocked by a mound of earth and begins just north of the route to the parking area. Take the overgrown grade for 0.6 mile to its junction with the steep jeep road just above the parking area.) To drive to the high parking area, turn left at the pipe and travel 0.6 mile to a turnout where a sign states Missouri Lake Trail ½.

Walk up the steep road to a diversion dam and a sign at the edge of the trees indicating the mileages to Missouri Lakes and Pass. (Forest Service maps show the trail number as 2003, not number 1903 as indicated by the sign.) Hike through woods and cross Missouri Creek on a log footbridge then wind steeply up near the rim of a rocky, steep-walled gorge. Near 1.0 mile recross the stream on a wide bridge where you will have a superb view up and down the gorge. Continue climbing steeply for 0.2 mile and come to the east edge of a large meadow. The grade generally is more moderate for the remaining distance to the lakes.

Walk along the north edge of the clearing then a short distance beyond the west end of the meadow travel along another narrow, rocky section of the gorge formed by Missouri Creek. Climb through a small, lush clearing and continue rising through open woods then walk near Missouri Creek for a short distance at 2.2 miles. Ford a small side stream and farther on come to a larger one. Climb steeply through increasingly alpine terrain to the east end of the basin that holds the lakes. Pass the junction on your left of the obscure path to the first of the lakes. The north shore is about 0.3 mile from the main trail and reaching it involves only 100 feet of elevation gain.

Continue on the main trail and traverse an open slope above the lowest lake. Wind up over the attractive timberline terrain of scattered trees, small rock outcroppings and grass for 0.2 mile to the largest of the lakes. Walk near the west shore at a gradual grade with many slight dips and climbs to its northwest end.

To reach flower-splashed Missouri Pass continue along the main trail to the end of the basin, passing the highest lake in the chain, and wind steeply up the basin wall.

"Friends"

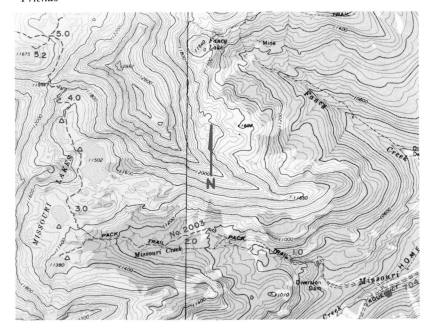

16 LONESOME LAKE

One day trip or backpack
Distance: 4.6 miles one way
Elevation gain: 1,550 feet
High point: 11,550 feet
Allow 2½ to 3 hours one way
Usually open July through September
Topographic map:
   U.S.G.S. Homestake Reservoir, Colo.
   7.5′   1970

One-half of the hike to Lonesome Lake is through the length of two immense meadows. Beyond the clearings the trail winds up through woods to the end of a lush, grassy basin below the lake. The final 0.4 mile is easy cross-country travel near or above timberline. This trip is the most southerly of the six in the Homestake area.

Drive on U.S. 24 ten miles south of Minturn or 11 miles north of Tennessee Pass to a sign stating Blodgett Campground, Gold Park and Trails to High Lakes. Turn southwest and travel on the unpaved, but smooth and mostly level, road for 10 miles to a signed junction below the Homestake Reservoir Dam. Unless you have a 4-wheel drive vehicle you probably will want to leave your car here.

Walk up the road to the left (southeast) for 0.4 mile to where you come to a water diversion pipe, several hundred yards beyond a drop in the road. Turn sharply left, cross a flat area and follow the road that climbs very steeply beside the pipe for one-quarter mile to the end of the spur road at a diversion dam.

Turn right and walk several yards toward a sign. Bear left (south) and follow cairns for several hundred feet across an open area at a slight angle away from the pond to the beginning of the obvious trail. Walk at a gradual grade through woods for 0.2 mile to the north end of the first long meadow. The intriguing and delightful blossoms of elephant heads are especially profuse here.

Travel along the west side for one mile to the far end then climb moderately in woods for a short distance. Cross a little side stream in an alpine setting of rock and grass and a few hundred feet farther come to the second long meadow. Walk just above its floor for one-half mile to the opposite end where some avalanche debris is scattered over the slope. Reenter woods and where you come to a small clearing keep along the left side, following a faint trail. Bear left again where the path is faint in the woods. Walk along the crest of a small grassy ridge. Near 3.1 miles the trail curves southwest and climbs more noticeably. Follow a circuitous route through woods to the end of a lush basin at 4.1 miles.

Note where the trail stops so you can locate the main route on your return. Although you can hike cross-country along either side of the basin, the traverse along the southeastern (left) wall is more direct. The density of the marsh marigold blossoms here equals that of the elephant heads in the lower meadows. Climb along one of the slopes toward the head of the basin for 0.2 mile then travel across a grassy bench, passing some tarns if you took the southeastern route, to the shore of the lake.

Campsite at Lonesome Lake

Fisherman at Lonesome Lake

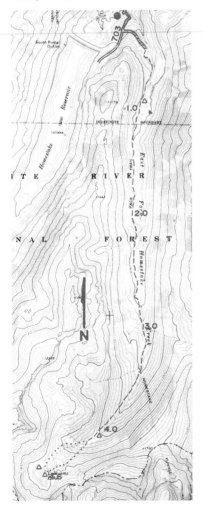

17

HENDERSON and COFFEEPOT PARKS

One day trip
Distance: 2 miles one way
Elevation gain: 1,310 feet
High point: 10,550 feet
Allow 1½ hours one way
Usually open June through September
Topographic map:
  U.S.G.S. Nast, Colo.
  7.5′   1970

Six delightful hikes (No's. 17 through 22) probe the Fryingpan River area east of Ruedi Reservoir. None climb steeply or are long and all but two visit one or more lakes. While hiking over the relatively gentle terrain of woods and many meadows it is always somewhat surprising to remember that the considerably more rugged Homestake area (No's. 11 through 16) is just beyond the ridges to the northeast.

Meadows frequently begin as lakes or areas of poor drainage. As sediment from the inlet streams fill the lake or marsh, grass starts to grow. After a meadow has been formed and conditions are favorable, trees begin to establish themselves.

Henderson and Coffeepot Parks are immense meadows and their grassy expanse is a pleasing change of scene from the usual destination of a pass, summit or lake. The first mile of the trail mostly is through aspen spiced with wild flowers and some rocky outcroppings and the second half, except for the parks, is in spruce forest.

Proceed on Colorado 82 to Basalt and at the west end of the community turn north on the road to Ruedi Dam. Drive 27 miles to the junction of a dirt road on the left marked by a sign pointing to Elk Wallow Campground. Turn left, leaving the paved surface, and drive four miles to a fork. Keep left and after 150 yards be watching for a small sign stating Henderson Park on the north bank. A small turnout on the south shoulder of the road provides parking for a few cars.

Wind up along a slope of grass and aspen to a bench with a few rock outcroppings. Travel at a more gradual grade then resume climbing over the sometimes rough terrain. Drop slightly then resume hiking uphill. During the first portion of the trip the wild flowers, including Mariposa lily, harebells, asters and green Indian paintbrush, are profuse in quantity and variety. Switchback up through a grove of aspen and at 0.9 mile, after the last turn, pass a small wooden trough on your left that collects water from a spring above the trail. Continue traversing up to a clearing, almost completely vegetated with false hellebore. Cross the small meadow and reenter woods, now composed of tall spruce. Traverse the forested slope then climb briefly, curve left and drop a few yards to near a stream. Walk parallel to the flow to the southwestern tip of Henderson Park.

Walk along the left (west) edge of the meadow for 100 yards to where two logs sprawl over the grass. Turn left and look for blazes that mark a wide trail heading west into the woods. After a few feet the trail turns sharply right and goes north through the forest near the edge of the clearing. Climb for 0.1 mile then descend for the same distance to the south end of smaller Coffeepot Park.

If you want to continue the hike, again keep left and walk along the edge of Coffeepot Park for 150 yards to the eight-foot-high stake that marks a well-defined trail into the woods. Travel on the level for about 150 feet then drop slightly. Traverse a more open, rocky slope above a small clearing then wind down for a few hundred yards to a lush meadow. The trail continues descending west to a junction at Last Chance Creek.

Henderson Park

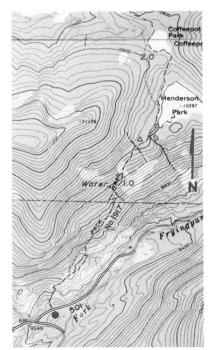

Trailside Spring

18 SAVAGE LAKES

One day trip or backpack
Distance: 2.5 miles one way
Elevation gain: 1,300 feet
High point: 11,180 feet
Allow 1 to 1½ hours one way
Usually open July through September
Topographic map:
   U.S.G.S. Nast, Colo.
    7.5′   1970

A merry stream flowing through an equally cheery slope of grass and wild flowers above the east shore of the lowest of the Savage Lakes is a charming spot to rest before making the short climb to a higher lake, exploring the area southwest of the lower one or just returning to the trailhead.

Drive on Colorado 82 to Basalt and at the west end of the community turn north on the road to Ruedi Dam. Proceed 27 miles to the junction of a dirt road on your left marked by a sign pointing to Elk Wallow Campground. Turn left, leaving the paved surface, and drive four miles to a fork. Keep left, pass the beginning of the route to Henderson and Coffeepot Parks (No. 17) after 150 yards, and go 3.1 miles to a sign on the left stating Savage Lakes Trail Parking at the beginning of the hike.

Gradually wind up through woods for a short distance then begin a moderately steep rise. After 0.2 mile the grade is less severe and eventually the route begins traveling parallel to the outlet creek from lower Savage Lake. Along one section a rocky cliff band borders the trail on the north. At 1.1 miles hop the stream and 100 yards farther recross the flow.

After a brief climb cross a small creek and immediately begin traveling up a short, very rocky stretch. The tread becomes smoother and the grade more moderate then the route comes to a lush, grassy clearing at the edge of the basin holding the lowest Savage Lake. Walk across the meadow, re-enter woods and after several yards look down to the lake. A picnic table and outhouse are in the woods 150 feet from the shore.

To reach the recommended lunch stop or to visit the higher lake drop to near the shore then turn left and follow one of the parallel paths along the northern side, the higher one being the preferable route. Walk over the grassy, sometimes rocky terrain, climbing slightly above the lake, to a small inlet stream. Cross it and wind up a path for a few hundred feet then where you come below a rock band on your left turn right and travel cross-country to the south. The nature of the terrain will funnel you to a spot above the lake. A third, considerably smaller member of the Savage Lakes family is 400 feet higher in the little basin to the east.

46

Lower Savage Lake

19 LYLE and MORMON LAKES

One day trip or backpack
Distance: 3 miles one way
Elevation gain: 980 feet; loss 250 feet
High point: 11,680 feet
Allow 2 hours one way
Usually open July through September
Topographic map:
  U.S.G.S. Nast, Colo.
  7.5'   1970

If you had to select the most scenic of the six hikes in the Fryingpan River area probably the trip to Lyle and Mormon Lakes would be the choice. Even the drive to the trailhead is exceptionally attractive. The trail travels up a broad valley of grass and scattered trees for the first 1.4 miles to a bench and Lyle Lake then traverses the head of a massive valley to the grassy and rocky bowl holding Mormon Lake. One of the many cross-country trips you could make across the inviting terrain is to the large tarn 0.4 mile and 300 feet above Mormon Lake to the southeast. More demanding would be the climb east from Lyle Lake to a crest due west of Turquoise Lake and Leadville.

Proceed on Colorado 82 to Basalt and at the west end of the community turn north on the road to Ruedi Dam. Drive 32.5 miles on the main road, passing the road to Norrie Colony after 28 miles, to a fork. Stay left on Road 105, after 100 yards come to the end of the pavement and keep left again, still on Road 105. Three miles farther stay right on the same road for eight miles to a sign stating Leadville and Hagerman Pass where a spur goes up to the left. One hundred feet farther along the main route is a turnout on the north. Park here.

Look for a small sign stating Lyle Lake 2 on the bank just southeast of the turnout. Walk to it, turn left and climb along a path for several yards to a road. Continue in the same direction you were heading, crossing the road, and begin traveling along an old track. Climb gradually along the gentle, predominantly grassy valley wall. Cross two small streams, drop slightly and climb the final distance to Lyle Lake. You can see the trail ahead climbing the slope above the middle of the Lake.

Paths go right or left around the shore—the former is shorter but involves crossing a small boulder field. Follow the trail over the crest of the slope and begin traversing at a gradual grade. Pass above some tarns you may want to visit now or on your return. Climb slightly over a small crest then wind down a rocky slope, losing about 100 feet of elevation. Conies make their homes beneath the rocks along this section. Resume traversing the wall at the valley's head then climb more noticeably to a grassy vale. The trail is faint beyond here so note landmarks where the tread stops so you can locate it on your return. Pass a tarn on your left then veer slightly left and come to an overlook 80 feet above Mormon Lake.

Tarn above Lyle Lake

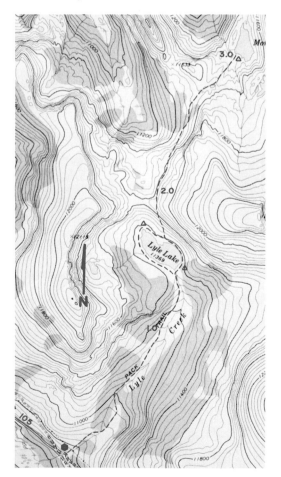

20 PORPHYRY MOUNTAIN

One day trip
Distance: 4.5 miles one way
Elevation gain: 2,415 feet
High point: 11,765 feet
Allow 2 to 2½ hours one way
Usually open late June through September
Topographic map:
 U.S.G.S. Meredith, Colo.
 7.5'   1970

The list of landmarks visible from the large summit of Porphyry Mountain reads like a "what's what" of north-central Colorado. Looking west then turning counterclockwise you can see the high peaks of western Colorado, Mount Sopris, Capitol Peak, Snowmass Mountain, Maroon Bells, Castle Peak, Aspen Mountain, Snowmass at Aspen and Aspen Highlands Ski Areas, the peaks of the Lincoln Creek drainage, the area near Independence Pass, Mount Massive, the Collegiate Range, almost the entire terrain comprising the Fryingpan River drainage, Mount of the Holy Cross and the area surrounding it, Crooked Creek Pass and Mount Thomas. However, even without the panorama at the end of the climb the hike through large meadows and deep woods to the summit is, in itself, scenic. Carry water as trail sources may be contaminated.

Drive on Colorado 82 to Basalt and at the western end of the community turn north on the road to Ruedi Dam. Proceed 28 miles to a sign pointing right to Norrie Colony. Turn right, cross the valley floor and climb a short distance to the settlement. Just beyond the first building (a shop) on your left joggle very slightly left and soon begin winding uphill on the wide, unpaved road. Two and three-quarter miles from Norrie come to a spur on your right identified by a sign stating Aspen-Norrie Trail. A few parking spaces are along the shoulder of the main road.

Walk along the roadbed for 0.2 mile to the north end of Twin Meadows, portions of which are used as a gravel pit and excess earth dump. Travel beside a stream and cross the clearing to a small sign on the western side stating Aspen-Norrie Trail. Curve left and follow the lower path through woods near the meadow. Resume walking along the edge of the grass then travel along an old road grade and at 1.1 miles come to a little clearing. You can see the trail climbing the low bank across the opening.

Climb along the old roadbed at a generally gradual grade through a forest of widely spaced trees. Where a signed trail leaves the road keep right on the path and continue upward. Traverse an open slope and rejoin the road. Resume climbing along the road that eventually narrows into a trail. Near 2.6 miles come to a meadow. Head toward a cluster of conifers upslope from a lone tree in the middle of the clearing. From this grove follow blazes and the path across the west side of the open area and into the trees. Climb steeply through dense woods for three-quarters mile to the crest of the ridge at Sawmill Park. From here you will have a preview of the scene from the summit: on the southwestern skyline are the Maroon Bells, Pyramid Peak, Loge Peak and the Aspen Highlands Ski Area.

Follow along the right (north) edge of the meadow for 120 yards to a road. Metal discs on trees identify the route. Walk north along the road for a short distance then begin a moderately steep climb. Near 3.9 miles where a faint spur continues straight, curve left on the main route, following the metal discs. Traverse west along the wooded slope just below the ridge crest for 0.2 mile then as the trees begin to thin wind up to the summit area. Pass a cabin and continue climbing to the remains of the downed lookout tower.

Sawmill Park

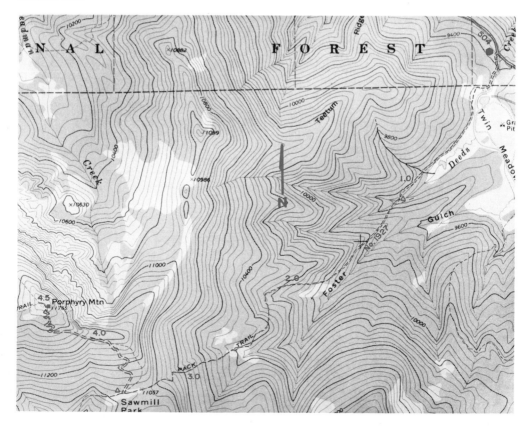

21 SAWYER LAKE

One day trip or backpack
Distance: 4.5 miles one way
Elevation gain: 1,500 feet
High point: 11,020 feet
Allow 2 hours one way
Usually open late June through September
Topographic map:
    U.S.G.S. Meredith, Colo.
    7.5′   1970

The hike to the wooded shore of Sawyer Lake travels through forests and across several large meadows. Although it is one of the two longest trips in the Fryingpan River area, the trail grade is gradual to moderate for the entire distance. Do not drink from any of the several streams you cross before 2.3 miles as they may be contaminated by grazing animals.

Proceed on Colorado 82 to Basalt and at the western end of the community turn north on the road to Ruedi Dam. Drive 28 miles to a sign pointing right to Norrie Colony. Turn right, cross the valley floor and climb a short distance to the settlement. Just beyond the first building (a shop) on your left turn very slightly left and soon begin winding uphill on the wide, unpaved road. Two and three-quarter miles from Norrie keep left where a spur goes right and 0.1 mile farther come to a sign stating Sawyer Lake 5. Parking spaces for a few cars are available along the shoulder.

Walk about 15 feet west of the sign to locate the beginning of the trail. Descend briefly then travel in deep woods near the western edge of Twin Meadows. Cross a stream, go through more open terrain of grass and trees to a second stream then just before entering woods cross a third flow. Begin climbing at a steady, moderate grade through lodgepole pine.

Come to a level stretch a few hundred feet long then resume climbing. The route crosses an old roadbed a few times then at 1.9 miles comes to a small ravine at a saddle. Go through the interesting formation to its east end at a meadow. Curve right and walk on the level along the west edge of the clearing that becomes considerably more extensive as you continue. Enter woods, hop a small stream and travel through the forest several yards from the clearing. Come to the southern end of the meadow and walk across the grass to some trail signs. A faint path goes northeast to Chapman Gulch and Campground.

Continue on the main trail into woods in the same direction you were heading and after several yards pass a camp and the remains of a cabin. Begin climbing and traverse two small clearings, traveling beside a stream to the second grassy slope. Although many side paths diverge from the trail, the main route is obvious.

At 3.5 miles leave the timber at a bench and climb gradually over an open, rocky saddle, traveling above two tarns that may dry up later in the summer. Drop slightly, cross a creek and climb out of the small gully. Traverse along the grassy slope, passing the remains of a tiny cabin. Enter woods and continue uphill. Cross a stream then travel along the east edge of a small clearing just before Sawyer Lake. The resident Clark nutcrackers may urge you to share your lunch with them.

Old cabin near Sawyer Lake

Sign at the second meadow

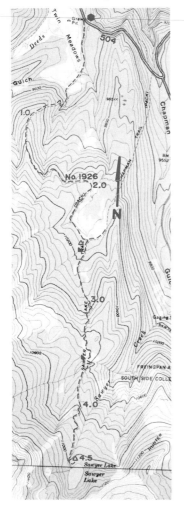

22 CHAPMAN LAKE

One-half day trip or backpack
Distance: 1 mile one way
Elevation gain: 200 feet
High point: 9,785 feet
Allow ½ hour one way
Usually open June through September
Topographic map:
  U.S.G.S. Meredith, Colo.
  7.5′   1970

Indian pond lily

The hike to Chapman Lake is the shortest hike in the Fryingpan River area and the second briefest in this guide. Much of the north end of the lake is covered with Indian pond lilies that reach their peak of blossoming around mid-July. Carry drinking water as none is available along the trail.

Drive on Colorado 82 to Basalt and at the western end of the community turn north on the road to Ruedi Dam. Proceed 28 miles to a sign pointing right to Norrie Colony. Turn right, cross the valley floor and climb a short distance to the settlement. Just beyond the first building (a shop) on your left turn slightly left and soon begin winding uphill on the wide, unpaved road. Two and three-quarter miles from Norrie keep left where a spur goes right and one mile farther turn right at a junction, following the sign to Chapman Lake Trail. Go 0.7 mile to a large turnout on your left where a somewhat obscure sign points to the trailhead at the north edge of the parking area.

Traverse up the rocky slope of small pines and scattered aspen at an irregular but always moderate grade for one-half mile to the edge of the broad, flat ridge crest. Drop slightly and wind through woods. Pass near the northern tip of a long meadow then continue through woods to the junction of a trail that heads east for 1.5 miles to Nast Lake. Keep right and decend gradually for 130 yards to the northeastern end of Chapman Lake. A good campsite is several yards farther along the trail.

54

Trail sign

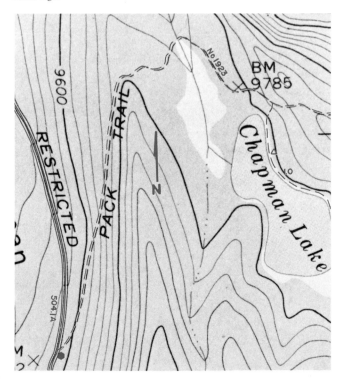

23 THOMAS LAKES

One day trip or backpack
Distance: 3.5 miles one way
Elevation gain: 1,600 feet
High point: 10,200 feet
Allow 2 hours one way
Usually open June through September
Topographic maps:
  U.S.G.S. Basalt, Colo.
  7.5′   1961
  U.S.G.S. Mount Sopris, Colo.
  7.5′   1961

The twin summits of massive, 12,953 foot high Mount Sopris dominate the landscape for those driving southeast of Glenwood Springs on Colorado 82. Thomas Lakes are tucked against the northeastern side of the mountain and energetic hikers could use the shores as a base camp for a climb of the peak. The hike is especially attractive in the fall when the aspen and oak are costumed in hues of yellow, gold and russet. Carry water as none is available along the trek.

Proceed 12 miles southeast of Glenwood Springs on Colorado 82 to the junction of Colorado 133. Turn south and drive three miles to a road on your left (east) identified by a sign pointing to Dinkle Lake. Turn left and after two miles come to the end of the paved road and keep right at a fork, following the sign to Dinkle Lake. The remaining distance is rough and steep in some places, but the road is passable. Four and one-half miles from the fork keep right again and two miles farther come to a cluster of signs at a fork. Keep right and park in the flat area between the two roads. If you have a 4-wheel drive vehicle you can continue another 1.7 miles.

Begin walking along the road to the south and west and after several yards where you come to a fork you can follow either branch, with the right one being somewhat shorter. Switchback left at 0.7 mile and continue uphill along the timbered slope. Keep left on the main road where a spur climbs at an acute angle to the right. Eventually, you will be able to see down onto Dinkle Lake and farther on the Sawatch Range is visible along the northeastern horizon. Travel across a treeless slope for one-third mile to a junction and space for parking if you have driven this far.

Keep right, as indicated by the sign pointing to Thomas Lake, and at the fork 150 yards from the junction you can follow either route: the left branch climbs through an aspen grove and the right one passes a viewpoint that affords far-ranging views to the east, northeast and north to the distinctive Flat Tops. Climb along the extremely rough road through woods of aspen and pine and other conifers. As you gain elevation the trees become less plentiful and are almost entirely evergreen. In contrast to the somewhat arid character found at the beginning of the hike, the scene is considerably more alpine in appearance.

At 3.2 miles pass a pond on your right and continue the remaining distance up to the most westerly of the Thomas Lakes. The best campsites are along the southeastern shore. To reach the other large lake, keep left on the spur road you pass just before reaching the lower one. Both summits of Mount Sopris that loom above to the south are the same height but the one on your right (west) appears higher.

East shoulder of Mt. Sopris

Thomas Lake

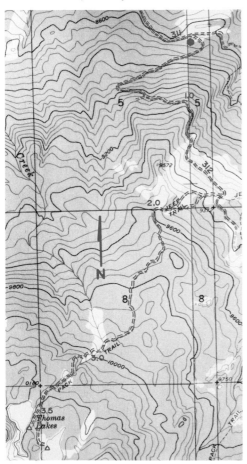

24 HELL ROARING CREEK

One day trip or backpack
Distance: 5.5 miles one way
Elevation gain: 4,870 feet
High point: 12,170 feet
Allow 4½ to 5½ hours one way
Usually open July through September
Topographic map:
   U.S.G.S. Redstone, Colo.
   7.5'   1960

This demanding hike ends at the crest of the northernmost portion of the Elk Mountains. The southeastern flank of Mount Sopris extends nearby to the north and more distant views include the Flat Tops, the Gore and Medicine Bow Ranges, the peaks around Independence Pass, Haystack Mountain, Capitol Peak, Snowmass Mountain, Treasury Ridge and Chair Mountain.

Drive on Colorado 82 to the junction of Colorado 133. Turn south and go 12.5 miles to a sign pointing left (east) to Avalanche and Janeway Campgrounds. Turn left and proceed three miles along the rough and sometimes steep dirt road, keeping left at the entrance to Janeway Campground, to the large parking area at the southeast end of Avalanche Campground. A sign and register several yards southeast of the turnout identifies the Avalanche Trail.

Walk in woods along a smooth trail and cross two side streams. Travel through some small grassy clearings and begin climbing more noticeably, veering away from Avalanche Creek. Level off near 2.0 miles and come to a junction at the saddle between a large outcropping and the main slope.

Turn left and look for a sign stating Capitol Creek 11. Walk southeast for several yards to the resumption of the well-defined tread. Climb extremely steeply in short switchbacks along the wooded slope. Near 2.7 miles the grade becomes considerably more moderate as it travels through a band of oak and curves into the side canyon holding Hell Roaring Creek. Traverse at a gradual grade, occasionally dropping slightly, then resume switchbacking up very steeply. Just beyond where the trail again levels off and descends briefly a side path on your right goes to a small flat place beside Hell Roaring Creek, a good place to rest.

Again climb steeply and pass through an aspen woods with some blowdown before coming to an open bench. Walk across the slabs of exposed rock and resume winding up through aspen, climbing steeply near the top of the grove. Traverse a slope of alternating sections of grass and trees.

Near 4.0 miles at a large grassy clearing where the tread stops contour at the same elevation (do not drop) and head for an opening between two trees with a patch of exposed earth beyond. At the trees the trail is obvious again. Continue traversing through grass and conifers. After hiking about 200 yards across the final clearing before the wooded head of the valley be looking for a switchback up to your left. Make the turn and traverse then climb for a few hundred feet to a grassy bench. Do not follow the cairns that mark a path to the west. Instead, turn right and look for a section of a path traversing up the left side of the swale ahead of you to the north. Walk to the path and follow it up to a notch. Veer slightly right and continue uphill. Where you come to timberline go over a small hump and look right for the obscure trail up to the unnamed pass above Williams Lake on the crest about two miles southeast from the viewpoint. If you want to visit the pass you also can reach it by walking along the crest from the end of the hike.

To reach the viewpoint head cross-country over the floor of the basin and climb the north wall. Veer right and continue climbing along the grassy, rolling slopes for 0.5 mile to the summit of the main ridge.

Small stream in the upper meadows

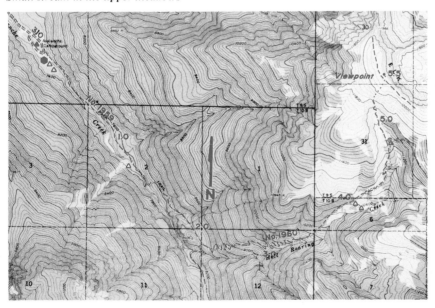

25 AVALANCHE PASS

One day trip or backpack
Distance: 5 miles one way
Elevation gain: 4,100 feet
High point: 12,100 feet
Allow 4½ to 5 hours one way
Usually open July through September
Topographic map:
U.S.G.S. Marble, Colo.
7.5′   1960

Five hikes (No's. 25 through 29) probe the slopes of the Crystal River Valley, in the past a scene of much mining activity. You will be on private property during portions of the hikes—be sure to respect the owners' rights.

The trail to Buckskin Basin and Avalanche Pass is the most scenic and remote of the trips in the Crystal River Valley area. During the latter half of July the slopes just below Buckskin Pass are smothered by spectacular wild flowers.

Proceed on Colorado 133 25 miles south of its junction with Colorado 82 to an unpaved road on your left marked by a sign pointing to Marble. Turn east, drive seven miles to the town and continue through the community to the first stop sign. Turn right and at the next junction turn left. After a few blocks turn left in front of the Beaver Creek Lodge and go west and north 0.2 mile to a road on your right where a sign states Carbonate Creek Trail. Off-road parking is available.

Walk east along the side road for 150 yards to a signed path on your left. Turn left, climb the bank, passing a sign stating you will be on private property for the next 1.5 miles, and wind up the arid, brushy slope. The tread is faint in a few places. After 0.5 mile travel below a road. Note where the trail ends as locating the route on the return can be a problem. Scramble up to the road and walk along it for 75 feet to where it curves right. Continue in the same direction you were heading, following the route identified by red bands of paint on the trees.

At 1.1 miles go through an open gate and rejoin the road. Keep left and walk along the bed for 150 feet; then where it curves right, keep straight into woods on an old roadbed. After several yards look for painted trees on your right and follow the path. Wind through woods, go through a gate and remeet the road. Keep left on the road then after a few yards turn left onto a path. A few yards farther turn right and travel parallel to the road then cross it and reenter woods as indicated by the red bands.

One hundred feet from the road cross Carbonate Creek, keep right at a fork several yards from the stream and begin climbing steeply. Pass through a clearing, cross a stream and continue climbing through aspen to the end of the dense woods near 2.5 miles. Walk along the grassy slope then before the trail reenters woods veer slightly right and walk cross-country at a gradual uphill angle to where you intercept the well-defined main trail.

Traverse the valley wall, going in and out of three successively smaller ravines between 3.0 and 3.5 miles. Pass a campsite at 3.9 miles and drop to an easy stream crossing. Do not obtain drinking water from this flow as sheep may be grazing in the basin above. Walk beside the creek for a short distance then recross it. Continue uphill along more lush, grassy terrain. Drop slightly then wind up above timberline. Near 4.6 miles come to a bench and travel at a considerably more moderate grade for several hundred yards then traverse up a short distance to a junction at Buckskin Pass. Turn left and climb the final one-quarter mile to narrow Avalanche Pass.

To make the recommended side trip into Buckskin Basin continue southeast from Buckskin Pass. Wind down to a stream crossing. A path goes right to a good campsite on a small ridge and the main trail continues downhill to a bench at the head of a large valley.

Capitol Peak from Avalanche Pass

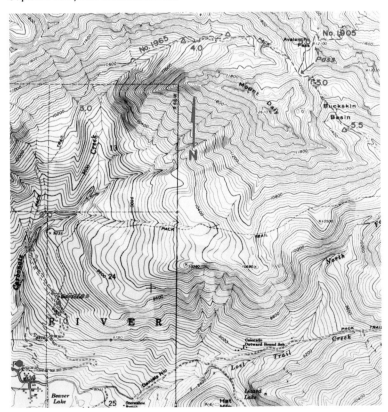

26 GENEVA LAKE

One day trip or backpack
Distance: 4 miles one way
Elevation gain: 2,000 feet
High Point: 10,950 feet
Allow 3½ to 4 hours one way
Usually open late June through September
Topographic map:
  U.S.G.S. Snowmass Mtn., Colo.
  7.5′   1960

The hike to very popular Geneva Lake, just inside the south-central boundary of the Maroon Bells-Snowmass Wilderness, begins at the old mining town of Crystal. Early in the 1870's several minerals were discovered in the Schofield area about 1.5 miles above to the southeast but because of transportation costs to Schofield, Crystal was developed instead. At its peak the community had a population of 650 and its buildings included 70 homes, several saloons and general stores, a schoolhouse, newspaper office, concentration mill and smelter. The town was almost deserted from 1893 on, except for a short burst of activity during 1916 and 1917. Today, several buildings remain and the old town and its setting are enjoyed by a few summer residents and many tourists on their way to Lead King Basin or over Schofield Pass.

Most of the road between the town of Marble and the beginning of the hike at Crystal is passable only to 4-wheel drive vehicles. Although the road is well-traveled and jeep drivers are most generous in offering rides, you cannot depend on a lift. The walk from where the road becomes steep east of Marble to Crystal would add about 4.5 miles one way to the hike.

Drive on Colorado 133 25 miles south of its junction with Colorado 82 to an unpaved road on your left marked by a sign pointing to Marble. Turn east, proceed seven miles to the town and continue through the community to the first stop sign. Turn right and at the next junction turn left. After a few blocks turn right at the junction by the Beaver Creek Lodge and drive 1.2 miles to a road on your right where a sign lists mileages to Lizard Lake and Crystal City. The angle of the road for 0.5 mile before this junction is very steep. Turn right and drive (or walk) at an irregular grade along the north wall of the canyon holding the Crystal River. One mile from the junction go along the south side of Lizard Lake, possibly the crater of an old volcano, and just before reaching Crystal pass picturesque Deadhorse Mill, one of the first built on the Crystal River. (A road continues from Crystal to the beginning of the trail proper but most of it is narrow and extremely rough.)

From Crystal walk up along the main road for 0.5 mile to a junction and turn left, following the arrows pointing to Geneva Lake and Lead King Basin. Continue climbing and after a few tenths mile travel above a deep gorge. Near 1.5 miles you can look northeast up to the rugged terrain in the vicinity of Trail Rider Pass. Cross a shallow side stream then farther on splash through another one.

A short distance beyond the second ford keep right at a fork then stay right again several yards farther. A plethora of signs, some pointing the wrong direction, are at these forks. Walk along the road, travel on a trail then rejoin the road and where a path diverges on the left, follow it. Where you remeet the road continue in the same direction, crossing the bed, and hike on the path to a bulletin board and the register at the beginning of the trail.

Traverse up the treeless slope, switchback and continue climbing, passing close to a side stream at 3.0 miles. Wind through an area of wooded benches above Geneva Falls to a little basin. Drop and climb slightly then come near the end of Geneva Lake. Several side paths descend to the shoreline. The main trail continues around the lake and climbs over Trail Rider Pass to Snowmass Lake. (No. 30).

Treasury Ridge

Old Deadhorse Mill at Crystal

27 MARBLE PEAK

One day trip
Distance: 4 miles one way
Elevation gain: 3,365 feet
High point: 11,314 feet
Allow 4 to 4½ hours one way
Usually open late June through September
Topographic map:
   U.S.G.S. Marble, Colo.
   7.5′   1960

The view from the summit of Marble Peak includes the long ridge of Treasure Mountain across the deep valley holding Yule Creek and south into the basin at the headwaters of North Anthracite Creek. The hike traverses open, grassy slopes for half its length and near the end of the trip you will have a few hundred yards of cross-country travel.

Proceed on Colorado 133 25 miles south of the junction of Colorado 82 and 133 to an unpaved road on your left marked by a sign pointing to Marble. Turn east and after seven miles pass the sign marking the west boundary of the town and continue on the main road to the first public spur on your right. This side road is just beyond the small, white Trading Post and before a larger, log General Store, both on your left. Turn right and go 200 feet to a parking area at the edge of the old marble mill. Signs remind you that you are on private property.

From the parking area continue along the road for several yards and cross a bridge over the Crystal River. Walk up the road for 0.3 mile to a sign on your right pointing to Raspberry and Yule Creeks. Keep right, leaving the road, and wind up along the sparsely vegetated slope. Soon enter aspen woods and continue climbing. Go in and out of a small ravine then in bushy terrain be watching for an unsigned fork in the trail. Curve left and continue climbing through aspen and an occasional clearing. (If you accidently take the wrong fork you soon will realize your mistake as the tread becomes faint then stops.) At 1.2 miles come to the junction of the trail to Raspberry Creek.

Keep left and travel through more aspen before entering a stand of large conifers. Just before the edge of the evergreens pass a dry camp on your left at 1.5 miles, go through one last grove of aspen and begin traversing the slope of flowers and tall grass. The blooms usually are their best during mid-July. At 1.9 miles cross over a saddle between the main wall and a small forested hill. You can look up to your destination along the next section of the traverse. Enter and leave a small ravine with a creek, cross a smaller flow and come to a severely eroded stream bed. Look for the resumption of the trail across the gully and scramble across to it.

Several yards from the wash begin climbing steeply through deep woods and where you come to an unsigned junction on the face of a ridge turn right and continue uphill. Soon begin traveling at a gradual grade along a mostly grassy, open slope. Drop to a broad saddle identified as Anthracite Pass.

Turn so you are facing the rocky face of the mountain ahead to the northwest. Look very slightly left for a corridor through the trees, go through it then bear right. The trail becomes increasingly well-defined beyond this point. Soon begin traversing an open slope. Come to the edge of a stand of timber, switchback left and traverse up more steeply. After a few hundred yards be watching for a switchback to the right and follow it. Make one more switchback to the left and traverse up the final distance to the summit ridge. Turn right and walk along the crest to the high point. Capitol Peak is visible far to the northeast, the route to the Skyline Mine (No. 29) is identifiable on the opposite side of Yule Creek Valley and you can look southeast up the valley to Yule Pass.

64

Ragged Mountain

Looking south from the summit

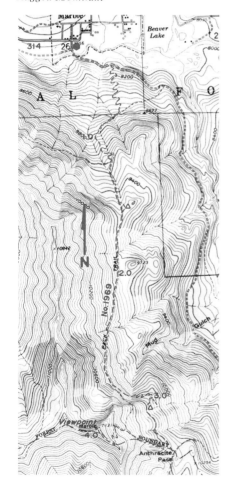

65

28 YULE MARBLE QUARRY

One day trip
Distance: 3.8 miles one way
Elevation gain: 1,500 feet
High point: 9,400 feet
Allow 2 hours one way
Usually open May through September
Topographic map:
   U.S.G.S. Marble, Colo.
     7.5'   1960

The Yule Marble Quarry was opened in 1905, thirteen years after the first marble in the area was extracted. The operation was named for George Yule, the first white man to discover and realize the value of the marble around Yule Creek. When the mill was built in 1906-08 it was the largest such plant in the world. The operation was closed from 1916 to 1922 then reopened until 1941 when it ceased operating permanently. Marble from the quarry was used for the Lincoln Memorial and the Tomb of the Unknown Soldier plus many buildings in Colorado, California, Nebraska and several other states.

The hike to the Yule Marble Quarry be-gins at the remains of the mill, torn down in 1943, and climbs along a jeep road to the edges of the three immense chambers. In addition to gazing into these awesome caverns you can make short side trips to the shell of the old powerhouse or to one of the tramway towers used to transport the marble blocks down to the mill. The quarry is a popular destination for those with 4-wheel drive vehicles so you will have much company if you hike on a weekend or holiday.

Drive on Colorado 133 25 miles south of its junction with Colorado 82 to an unpaved road on your left marked by a sign pointing to Marble. Turn left and after seven miles pass the sign marking the western boundary of the town. Continue on the main road to the first public spur on your right. This side road is just beyond the small, white Trading Post and before a larger, log General Store, both on your left. Turn right and go 200 feet to a parking area at the edge of the old marble mill. Signs remind you that you are a guest on private property.

From the parking area continue along the road for several yards and cross a bridge over the Crystal River. Walk up the road for 1.9 miles, passing the beginning of the trail to Marble Peak (No. 27) after 0.3 mile, to a spur heading gradually downhill on your left for 0.4 mile to the remains of the powerhouse and beyond to the Skyline Mine (No. 29).

Keep right on the main road and continue climbing. Cross two shallow side streams and at 3.0 miles walk in and out of a side canyon. Where the road curves sharply south you can look southwest to the summit of Marble Peak. Walk above boisterous Yule Creek along the west wall of a rocky, attractive little gorge. At a washout, scramble over the debris for several yards to the resumption of the road and walk to a flat area at creek level. The road crosses the flow to the tramway tower remains.

To reach the quarry keep right and climb steeply for 200 yards to the edge of the middle chamber. To see into the upper chamber turn left and climb 150 feet along a road. Also, you can scramble down the ravine to the right (north) of the middle chamber then climb to the edge of the third one where you can look through the other two. A tunnel from the bottom of the ravine goes to the ice covered floor of the northern-most chamber.

Inside the quarry

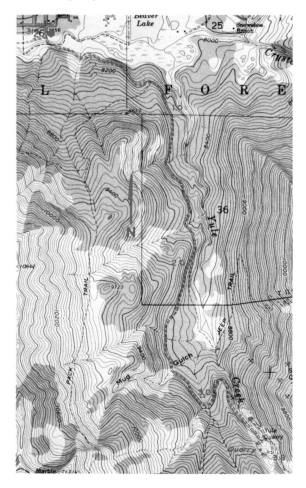

29 SKYLINE MINE

One day trip
Distance: 5.5 miles one way
Elevation gain: 3,875 feet
High point: 11,775 feet
Allow 4½ to 5 hours one way
Usually open late June through September
Topographic map:
 U.S.G.S. Marble, Colo.
 7.5′   1960

The climb to the Skyline Mine (also called Little Darling Mine) near the west end of the long ridge that forms Treasure Mountain is the most demanding of the five hikes in the Crystal River Valley area. During the ascent through woods and steep meadows you will have views across Yule Creek Valley to the light colored slopes of Marble Peak (No. 27) and near the end of the trip you can see north to Capitol, Hagerman and Snowmass Peaks. Note: Beyond the 3.5 mile point the road is open *only* to hikers. Vehicles of any type are prohibited.

Proceed on Colorado 133 25 miles south of its junction with Colorado 82 to an unpaved road on your left marked by a sign pointing to Marble. Turn left and after seven miles pass the sign identifying the west boundary of the town and continue on the main road to the first public spur on your

right. This side road is just beyond the small white Trading Post and before a larger, log General Store, both on your left. Turn right and go 200 feet to a parking area at the edge of the old marble mill. Signs remind you that you are a guest on private property.

From the parking area continue along the road for several yards and cross a bridge over the Crystal River. Walk up the road, passing the beginning of the trail to Marble Peak after 0.3 mile, for 1.9 miles to a spur heading gradually downhill on your left. (Do not take the previous drive on your left that drops steeply.) At the correct junction a road on the left climbs several yards to a small, flat spot. The main road to the right continues 1.9 miles to the Yule Marble Quarry (No. 28).

Walk down the road for 0.4 mile to a bridge over Yule Creek. This is the last source of water along the hike. Go to the concrete shell of the powerhouse for the tramway that carried the marble blocks from the Yule Quarry to the mill and follow the road that climbs to the northeast. Traverse the slope of aspen, switchback right and make another long traverse. Begin a series of short, moderately steep switchbacks and come to a large meadow on the hillside. Wind up through the open area and enter a stand of large, widely-spaced conifers. In this last section you can look southeast up to the saddle where the mine is located.

At 4.8 miles come to the lower edge of a rocky slope above a boulder-filled basin and curve left, following the main road. After a short distance curve right and traverse the rocky slope then reenter woods and continue climbing. At 5.4 miles where a spur goes left to the remains of a large cabin keep straight (right) on the main road and drop for 0.1 mile to the entrance to the mine.

The peak to the south above the saddle, instead of a high point, actually only is an outcropping on the lower portion of the ridge forming Treasure Mountain. If you want to make a side trip to it you can continue 0.5 mile farther along the road to near the top. This would involve an additional 500 feet of climbing. To view the peaks to the north return to the spur below the cabin at 5.4 miles and follow it for a few yards then turn left and climb several more yards to the crest.

Mine entrance tunnel

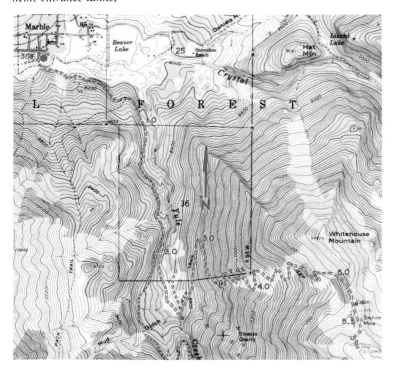

30 SNOWMASS LAKE

One day trip or backpack
Distance: 8.5 miles one way
Elevation gain: 2,585 feet
High point: 10,985 feet
Allow 4 to 5 hours one way
Usually open July through September
Topographic maps:
   U.S.G.S. Capitol Peak, Colo.
   7.5′   1960
   U.S.G.S. Snowmass Mtn., Colo.
   7.5′   1960

The hike to Snowmass Lake is one of the most popular trips in the Maroon Bells-Snowmass Wilderness. Although the lake itself is an entirely satisfactory destination, those desiring a more extended trek can continue southwest over Trail Rider Pass to Geneva Lake (No. 26) or southeast over Buckskin Pass (No. 33) to Maroon Lake. A 24.6 mile loop can be made by following the route over Buckskin Pass then climbing over Willow Pass to Willow Lake (No. 32) and returning to your starting point along Trail No. 31.

Drive on Colorado 82 to the community of Snowmass, 14 miles west of Aspen and 28 miles east of Glenwood Springs. Turn south at the sign stating Forest Access Road and after two miles keep left, following the sign pointing to Snowmass Campground. Two miles farther the pavement ends but the road surface is good and the grade continues to be moderate for the remaining distance. Travel an additional eight miles, pass the entrance to Snowmass Campground and after several yards turn right at a junction. Go the final 0.5 mile to a large parking area at the road's end. (A shorter approach is possible from the Aspen area but it involves a steep downgrade. Drive six miles

west of Aspen to the road to Snowmass Village. Turn south and after six miles, just before curving left to Upper Snowmass Village, keep right onto an unpaved road at the sign pointing to Lift 5. Travel 2.5 miles to the junction where the sign points to Snowmass Trails ½, turn left and go to the parking area.)

Go through the metal gate at the west side of the parking area and walk along a level road through pasture and woods for 0.6 mile then follow a trail on your left identified by a sign pointing to Snowmass Lake and Capitol Creek. Climb slightly and travel above more pastures. Walk on the level past a huge beaver pond, go through a second gate then keep left at the junction of the trail to Capitol Creek.

Pass through a third gate then after 100 feet enter a dense stand of aspen and come to a large bulletin board. Climb gradually through woods, crossing one open slope, and at 4.0 miles come to the junction of the rugged, unimproved hiker's trail to Pierre Lakes. Keep left then curve left, temporarily leaving Snowmass Creek, and wind up along the rocky trail. Come to a view of Bear Creek cascade across the broad valley. Traverse the canyon wall then, at 5.1 miles, walk close to Snowmass Creek where a few good campsites are above the trail.

Leave the stream again then after two-thirds mile traverse a rocky canyon wall and come to another large beaver pond. Walk around its eastern side and pass through a dense stand of timber. Travel above a meadow where Snowmass Creek placidly meanders, then along the valley floor to the bank of the creek. Turn left and follow a trail through the tall bushes for about 50 feet to a side path to a log dam across the flow.

Climb the opposite bank for a few yards to the main route, turn left and resume hiking on the well-graded trail. Wind around Snowmass Ponds then switchback twice. Climb in woods at a moderate grade, cross a small side stream then pass through a clearing. Beyond the small meadow keep right (straight) where an unsigned trail goes left. Climb along the wall of a narrow ravine just before coming to Snowmass Lake.

To reach Trail Rider or Buckskin Passes cross the footbridge across the outlet creek about 100 feet from the shore and walk a few hundred feet to a signed three-way junction.

Hagerman Peak and Snowmass Lake

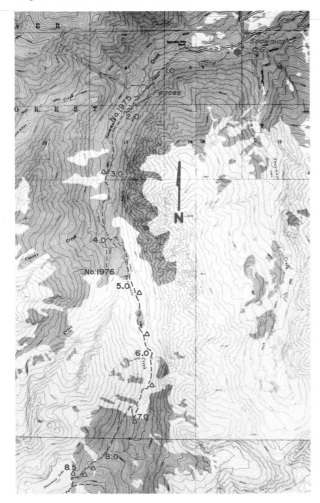

31 EAST SNOWMASS PASS and WILLOW LAKE

One day trip or backpack
Distance: 9 miles one way
Elevation gain: 4,300 feet; loss 900 feet
High point: 12,700 feet
Allow 5½ to 7 hours one way
Usually open July through September
Topographic maps:
 U.S.G.S. Highland Peak, Colo.
 7.5'   1960
 U.S.G.S. Maroon Bells, Colo.
 7.5'   1960

Willow Lake can be reached either from Willow Pass (No. 32) or from the north over East Snowmass Pass. This latter route climbs through woods for two miles then travels up a long valley to the Pass before dropping into the high, rolling basin that holds the lake. A 24.6 mile scenic loop is possible by continuing west from Willow Lake over Willow and Buckskin Passes (No. 33) then descending to Snowmass Lake and returning along the route described in Trail No. 30.

Proceed on Colorado 82 to the community of Snowmass, 14 miles west of Aspen and 28 miles east of Glenwood Springs. Turn south at the sign stating Forest Access Road and after two miles keep left, following the sign pointing to Snowmass Campground. Two miles farther the pavement ends but the road surface is good and the grade continues to be moderate for the remaining distance. Travel an additional eight miles, pass the entrance to Snowmass Campground and after several yards turn right at a junction. After 100 yards cross a bridge and 100 feet farther come to a sign identifying the beginning of the East Snowmass Trail. If no parking spaces are available along the shoulder you can continue to the large parking area at the road's end. (A shorter approach is possible from the Aspen area but it involves a steep downgrade. Drive six miles west of Aspen to the road to Snowmass Village. Turn south and after six miles, just before curving left to Upper Snowmass Village, keep right onto an unpaved road at the sign pointing to Lift 5. Travel 2.5 miles to the junction where the sign points to Snowmass Trails ½ and turn left to the parking spot.

Climb along the rocky side road and continue on it as it switchbacks right. Farther on, where a road comes from the right, continue in the same direction you were heading. Switchback right again then where the main road forks with one branch climbing to the left, keep straight (right). After several yards the bed narrows into a trail. Traverse uphill, curve sharply left then farther on walk on the level through an aspen grove. At its end near 1.0 mile come to a sign pointing right to Willow Lake and a few yards beyond the sign follow the trail that goes right. Traverse through woods, passing through another grove of aspen and lush grass.

Begin climbing more noticeably, make one set of short switchbacks and at 2.0 miles come to a gate. Meander up along the rolling, grassy treeless slope for one mile then switchback twice. Traverse the valley wall, crossing a few small side streams and a stretch of avalanche debris before entering a large grove of conifers at 3.5 miles. The grade becomes more gradual and the route passes through a few swampy areas. At a cairn where the trail forks turn right and climb steeply for a short distance then switchback left once and travel through more open woods. Traverse along the side of a grassy knoll then enter the final stand of timber.

Near 5.1 miles reach timberline and begin the two mile traverse along the grassy wall to the pass. Although irregular and even dropping at times, the grade is never severe. Sheep may be grazing on the valley floor or along walls so be careful where you obtain drinking water. From the narrow pass where you can see Willow Lake descend along the basin wall to the undulating floor. Keep left at the junction of the trail over Willow Pass and continue for 1.0 mile to Willow Lake. From the Viewpoint on the basin rim you can look 2,500 feet down onto Maroon Lake.

72

Fence at the first clearing

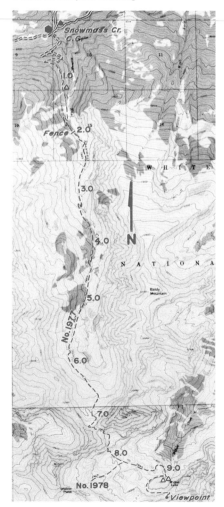

32 WILLOW LAKE

One day trip or backpack
Distance: 6.6 miles one way
Elevation gain: 3,000 feet; loss 800 feet
High point: 12,590 feet
Allow 4 to 4½ hours one way
Usually open July through September
Topographic map:
U.S.G.S. Maroon Bells, Colo.
7.5'   1960

The view across Maroon Lake to the distinctly stratified faces of the Maroon Bells is one of the most popular and accessible scenic attractions in the Colorado Rockies. Three strenuous hikes, No's. 32, 33 and 34, begin from Maroon Lake and follow the same route for the first 1.4 miles to a junction at Crater Lake. The East Maroon Creek Trail (No. 35) that begins along the road to Maroon Lake travels up a long valley toward East Maroon Pass. You can enjoy an overview of the main Maroon Creek Valley with the Maroon Bells at its head from the observation area on Loge Peak (No. 36).

Willow Lake lies at the east end of an immense, high, treeless basin. You can shorten the trip by four miles and avoid the 800 feet of elevation loss by stopping at narrow Willow Pass where you will have a fine view of the basin and lake. A side trip to Buckskin Pass (No. 33) from the 3.7 mile point would add 600 feet of elevation gain and a total of two miles. A second trail (No. 31) from the north that follows East Snowmass Creek also has Willow Lake as its destination.

Do not plan to camp along the trail to Crater Lake or anywhere within a radius of 0.5 mile from this lake as overnight stays in this area are prohibited.

Drive 0.5 mile west of Aspen on Colorado 82 to a road on the south side of the highway identified by a sign stating Maroon Lake and Ashcroft. Turn south and immediately come to a fork. Keep right and go nine miles then travel through Maroon Lake Campground to the large parking area above Maroon Lake at the end of the road.

Follow one of the several paths down across the open slope to the north shore of Maroon Lake. Head southwest, keeping right at the junction of the Beaver Trail, and climb gradually through an aspen grove. After passing the sign marking the Wilderness boundary the trail begins rising more noticeably and the surface becomes rocky. Hike through an open area and pass a few benches and a bulletin board. Beyond this rest area the trail curves left and makes a short set of switchbacks. Walk through a rocky bowl then begin dropping slightly above Crater Lake and at 1.4 miles come to the junction of the trail to West Maroon Pass (No. 34).

Keep right and wind up the slope then traverse at a moderately steep grade. Make a set of short switchbacks and enter a small side valley. Near 1.9 miles begin traversing the ravine formed by Minnehaha Creek. Climb in several switchbacks of irregular length then enter deep woods and travel on the level for a short distance before leaving the timber and fording Minnehaha Creek. Wind up through the alpine setting then travel through a small swale beside a stream to timberline. If you find evidence that sheep have been grazing beyond here do not drink from any of the streams you will be passing. Climb in six short switchbacks and come to the junction of the trail to Buckskin Pass.

Keep straight (right) and traverse up the wall of the bowl then climb in several short switchbacks. Cross a shallow stream and continue uphill into a grassy, hummock-filled bowl below Willow Pass. Follow the trail to the northeast end of the basin then curve right and traverse up the rocky wall. Switchback left then just below the crest make a few short switchbacks and come to Willow Pass.

To reach Willow Lake wind down from the Pass then hike across the basin for 0.3 mile to the junction with Trail No. 1977. Keep right and continue downhill, passing several small tarns, to the north shore of the lake.

74

Willow Pass

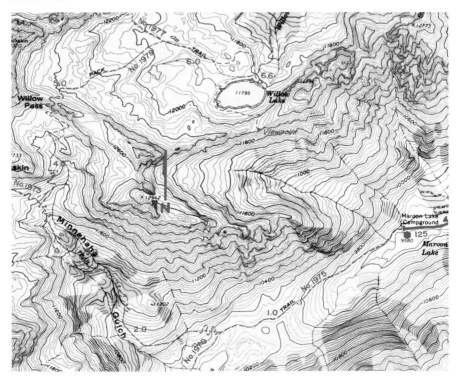

33 BUCKSKIN PASS

One day trip
Distance: 4.7 miles one way
Elevation gain: 2,900 feet
High point: 12,462 feet
Allow 3 to 3½ hours one way
Usually open July through September
Topographic map:
    U.S.G.S. Maroon Bells, Colo.
    7.5′   1960

From the knife-edge crest of Buckskin Pass you will have a view west across a broad valley to Snowmass Lake (No. 30) and the two-horned summit of Snowmass Mountain. The hike follows the route to Willow Lake (No. 32) for the first 3.7 miles and with an additional 800 feet of elevation gain and a total of two miles you can climb to Willow Pass and look over an immense, treeless rolling basin to the circular lake.

Proceed 0.5 mile west of Aspen on Colo-

rado 82 to a road on the south side of the highway identified by a sign stating Maroon Lake and Ashcroft. Turn south and immediately come to a fork. Keep right, drive nine miles and go through Maroon Lake Campground to the large parking area at the end of the road.

Follow one of the several paths down across the open slope to the north shore of Maroon Lake. Head southwest, keeping right at the junction of the Beaver Trail, and climb gradually through a grove of aspen. After passing the sign marking the Wilderness boundary the trail begins rising more noticeably and the surface becomes rocky. Go through an open area where you can see Pyramid Peak above to the south and pass a few benches and a bulletin board that holds warnings for potential climbers. Beyond this rest area the trail curves left and makes a short set of switchbacks. Walk through a rocky bowl where many large, furry marmots and appealing little conies make their homes. Begin dropping slightly above Crater Lake and at 1.4 miles come to the junction of the trail to West Maroon Pass (No. 34).

Keep right and wind up the slope then traverse at a moderately steep grade along the rocky trail. The surface soon becomes smooth and the trail makes a set of short switchbacks and enters a small side valley. Near 1.9 miles begin traversing high along the ravine formed by Minnehaha Creek. Climb in several switchbacks of irregular length then enter woods and travel on the level for a short distance before leaving the timber and fording Minnehaha Creek.

Wind up through the alpine setting then travel through a small swale beside a stream to timberline. If you find evidence that sheep have been grazing beyond here do not drink from any of the streams you will be passing. Climb in six short switchbacks and come to the junction of the trail to Willow Lake at the edge of a huge, grassy bowl. You probably will want to stop at this attractive spot to enjoy the fine views of Pyramid Peak, the Maroon Bells and Buckskin Pass.

Keep left, as indicated by the sign pointing to Snowmass Lake, and climb at a gradual, steady grade in nine switchbacks of varying lengths for the final 0.9 mile to Buckskin Pass. Snowmass Lake is four miles away by trail.

North Maroon Peak from the summit of Buckskin Pass

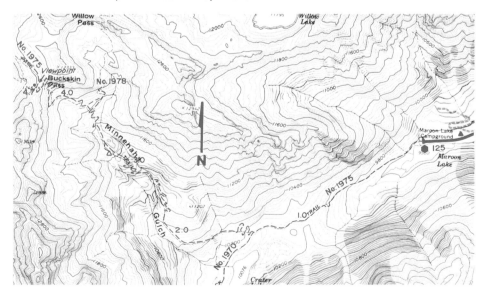

34 WEST MAROON PASS

One day trip or backpack
Distance: 6.3 miles one way
Elevation gain: 2,950 feet
High point: 12,500 feet
Allow 3½ to 4 hours one way
Usually open July through September
Topographic map:
   U.S.G.S. Maroon Bells, Colo.
   7.5'   1960

Drive 0.5 mile west of Aspen on Colorado 82 to a road on the south side of the highway identified by a sign stating Maroon Lake and Ashcroft. Turn south and immediately come to a fork. Keep right and go nine miles then travel through Maroon Lake Campground to the large parking area above Maroon Lake at the end of the road.

Follow one of the several paths down across the open slope to the north shore of Maroon Lake. Head southwest, keeping right at the junction of the Beaver Trail, and climb gradually through a grove of aspen. After passing the sign marking the Wilderness boundary the trail begins rising more noticeably and the surface becomes rocky. Pass through an open area where you can see Pyramid Peak above to the south and pass a few benches and a bulletin board that holds warnings for potential climbers. Beyond this rest area the trail curves left and makes a short set of switchbacks. Walk through a rocky bowl where many vocal marmots and conies make their homes then begin dropping slightly above Crater Lake and at 1.4 miles come to the junction of the trail to Buckskin Pass and Willow Lake.

Keep left and walk near the west shore of Crater Lake through grass and willows. Enter a dense stand of conifers then resume traveling in the open and traverse up the side of a massive scree slope. Descend slightly to the south end of the rocky area and walk at a gradual grade over terrain of scree, grass, brush and trees before crossing a small side stream and hiking through an area of willows. Travel beside West Maroon Creek, veer away from it for a short distance, then at 3.2 miles ford the flow.

After following the same route as the hikes to Willow Lake (No. 32) and Buckskin Pass (No. 33) for the first 1.4 miles, the trail over West Maroon Pass turns south and begins the five-mile-long valley walk to the rocky, narrow crest. Near the beginning of the trek you will be traveling between Pyramid Peak and the much-photographed Maroon Bells and from the destination you can look west over an emerald green basin toward the South Fork of the Crystal River and beyond to Treasure and Chair Mountains.

Since the route fords West Maroon Creek twice, the hike is best done after the beginning of July when the stream is not so swollen. Do not plan to camp along the trail to Crater Lake or anywhere within a radius of 0.5 mile from the lake as overnight stays in this area are prohibited.

Climb for a few hundred yards then travel at a gradual grade on a smooth surface for one mile to the second crossing. You may find some rocks on which to hop across several yards upstream. Resume a moderate climb along the valley wall. Trees and bushes become sparse and soon you will be traveling above timberline. At 5.0 miles curve slightly west into a large, grassy basin and hike over the irregular terrain with a few slight drops. Wind through a rocky area at 6.0 miles for a short distance then begin a steady traverse up the wall of red rock below West Maroon Pass. From the crest the trail heads northwest toward Frigidaire Pass and west down to Schofield Basin.

The Maroon Bells after first snowfall

35 EAST MAROON CREEK TRAIL

One day trip or backpack
Distance: 4.2 miles one way
Elevation gain: 700 feet; loss 570 feet
High point: 9,700 feet
Allow 2 hours one way
Usually open June through September
Topographic map:
U.S.G.S. Maroon Bells, Colo.
7.5′   1960

While traversing the grassy, aspen-dotted wall of the broad valley holding East Maroon Creek you will have views of the less familiar east side of distinctive Pyramid Peak, a companion to the Maroon Bells. The trail passes above several beaver ponds, some with lodges, and most of the grade is gradual.

Although the trail is described only to a beaver pond at 4.2 miles, those wanting a longer hike or backpack can continue along the established route to East Maroon Pass, five miles farther and 2,100 feet higher. From the Pass a trail descends past Copper Lake to Gothic. Also, trails go from below the north and south sides of East Maroon Pass to Copper Pass and from the latter you could traverse to Triangle Pass and descend to Conundrum Hot Springs (No. 37).

Proceed 0.5 mile west of Aspen on Colorado 82 to a road on the south side of the highway identified by a sign stating Maroon Lake and Ashcroft. Turn south and immediately come to a fork. Keep right and drive nine miles, passing a sign marking another —less desirable—trailhead for the hike, to a sign on your left stating Maroon Creek Trail and listing several mileages. A large parking area is across the road. The trailhead is several hundred yards before the entrance to Maroon Lake Campground.

Descend through aspen and grass to a bridge over West Maroon Creek. Continue downhill beside the flow, that is partially underground along this stretch, through deep timber. At 0.6 mile begin traversing more open, grassy terrain. Climb and drop over a small hump and cross East Maroon Creek on a bridge. Climb, keeping right where the trail forks, and continue up for a short distance to an old road. Turn right, walk through an attractive aspen grove for 0.5 mile and come to the edge of the woods.

Traverse the open, grassy slope and cross a shallow side stream that is a good spot for a snack stop. Walk along the valley wall, occasionally passing beneath scattered evergreens and aspen. Hike above some beaver ponds, cross another side stream and continue along the treeless slope above a huge beaver pond with a lodge. Cross a third side creek and travel above two more ponds, then climb more noticeably.

The trail resumes its gradual grade as it travels through another pleasing aspen grove. At 4.0 miles be watching for a road that goes downhill on your right. Descend, then veer left and walk to an area of several campsites near the edge of yet another beaver pond.

The Beaver Ponds

Aspen Grove

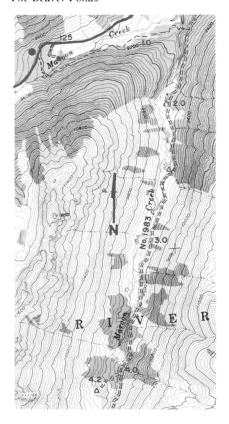

36 LOGE PEAK

One day trip
Distance: 3.8 miles one way
Elevation gain: 3,625 feet
High point: 11,675 feet
Allow 3½ to 4½ hours one way
Usually open late June through September
Topographic map:
U.S.G.S. Aspen, Colo.
7.5′   1960

Taking the chairlift to the summit of Loge Peak certainly is easier and faster than climbing to the top, but those who use the mechanical method rather than their own power miss, among other benefits, enjoyment of the many wild flowers, the closeup view of marmots and a patch of wild strawberries. From the summit you will have a good sighting up Maroon Creek Valley to the Maroon Bells, Maroon Lake and Pyramid Peak in addition to views in all other directions. Except for one short, welcome level stretch the grade is severe, but the grassy slopes make scenic, comfortable resting places.

For those who feel the climb to Loge Peak is not strenuous enough, the hike can be extended for another mile with 945 feet of elevation gain to the summit of Highland Peak along the ridge to the south. In case you want to take the lift one way, in the past it has operated Thursdays through Mondays, 9 to 4 o'clock. Carry water as none is available along the hike.

Drive 0.5 mile west of Aspen on Colorado 82 to a road on the south side of the highway identified by a sign stating Maroon Lake and Ashcroft. Turn south and immediately come to a fork. Keep right and go one mile to a sign stating Aspen Highlands Ski Area. Turn left into the huge parking area.

Walk to the east side of the parking lot and climb the few steps to the various shops. Continue straight and pass between tennis courts, veer right and begin climbing the treeless, grassy ski run. You will hear, and probably see, marmots as you gain elevation. Be careful not to step into any of their deep holes. Come to a bench at 0.5 mile where a large map identifies the many runs. Veer right and continue up a run for another 0.4 mile to a second bench where you will have a view of the Maroon Bells.

Follow the gradually graded roadbed along the crest, first walking through aspen then conifers. Travel beside the base of a rock wall on your left and come to a small grassy bowl. Bear right, leaving the road, and hike across the grass toward the buildings and chairlift you can see ahead. Wild strawberries are abundant here and, usually, will be succulent late in July.

Pass the buildings near the end of the lift at 2.1 miles and continue climbing, generally paralleling the next higher lift on your right. A picnic area and outhouse are located at the upper end of this latter lift. Resume climbing in the same direction along a narrow ridge and pass a stone monument marking the grave of Fred Iselin, a famous long-time Aspen ski instructor. Meet a road and turn left. You probably will feel you have done enough steep climbing for one day and welcome its more moderate grade.

Switchback up the road for 0.5 mile to the upper end of the last chair. A few hundred feet before the terminus you can leave the road and follow a path up to the right. A nature trail winds up the final one-quarter mile to the summit. An obvious path heads south from the uppermost terminus along the ridge crest and up to the summit of Highland Peak.

The grave of Fred Iselin

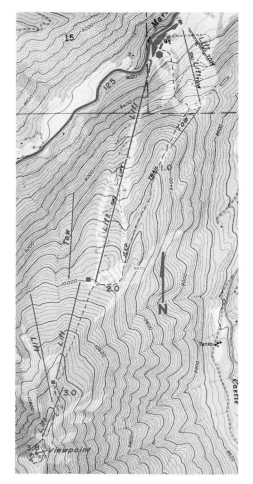

37 CONUNDRUM HOT SPRINGS

One day trip or backpack
Distance: 8.5 miles one way
Elevation gain: 2,500 feet
High point: 11,200 feet
Allow 4½ to 5 hours one way
Usually open July through September
Topographic maps:
U.S.G.S. Hayden Peak, Colo.
7.5'   **1960**
U.S.G.S. Maroon Bells, Colo.
7.5'   **1960**

The long but gently-graded trail up a broad valley to the pools at Conundrum Hot Springs is the most demanding of the four trips in the Ashcroft area just south of Aspen. Two of the other hikes that begin from the Ashcroft Road climb to lakes (No's. 38 and 39) and the fourth ends at Pearl Pass (No. 40).

If you do the hike to Conundrum Hot Springs in mid-July you probably will think almost every wild flower that thrives in the Colorado Rockies is represented some place along the route. Backpackers wanting a longer trip can follow a rugged hiker's trail over Electric Pass to Cathedral Lake (No. 39) or go over Triangle and Copper Passes and return down the East Maroon Creek Valley (No. 35).

Because of the avalanche danger and the three fords the trip should not be attempted early in the season. Due to extreme overuse of the area surrounding the pools, no overnight camping is allowed within 1.0 mile of the hot springs. Forest Service personnel patrol the area to enforce this regulation.

Proceed 0.5 mile west of Aspen on Colorado 82 to a road on the south side of the highway where a sign states Maroon Lake and Ashcroft. Turn south and immediately meet a fork. Keep left and drive five miles to a road on your right that may be designated by a small sign stating Trail 1981. Turn right and go downhill for a few hundred yards then follow the very rough, but passable, road for 1.5 miles through *private property* to a turnout for parking on your left just beyond the edge of the trees.

Follow the road as it repeatedly drops and climbs along the valley wall. Near 1.6 miles keep left on the main route where a spur goes downhill. Come to a meadow and pass a cabin, cross a shallow side stream and traverse a second clearing. Hike generally uphill through woods and clearings then near 2.9 miles travel near Conundrum Creek and come to the first ford. A log is across the flow several yards upstream. Continue south along the road and where it curves left keep straight on a short path to avoid a swampy stretch. Come to a treeless section of the valley floor and stay on the road to its abrupt end at 4.0 miles.

Traverse up a slope of aspen then begin traveling along grassy, brushy terrain and cross a side stream. Continue along the generally open terrain, crossing two more side streams and a few fingers of woods. Near 5.9 miles climb more noticeably for a short distance then drop gradually for several hundred feet to the second ford of Conundrum Creek. Just beyond the ford pass Silver Dollar Pond on your left then enter woods and come to the junction of the path over Electric Pass.

Turn right and after a short traverse above a marshy meadow walk on the level through woods to the third ford at 6.5 miles. Hike through woods and open areas and pass near the north and west edges of a swamp. Go through a series of brushy areas, woods and clearings then begin climbing more noticeably in a denser forest, crossing a few side streams. Near 8.1 miles the trees become more sparse and the route crosses a creek flowing down a little ravine. Travel parallel to a deep, rocky gorge formed by Conundrum Creek on your left then bear slightly right and come to a guard station. Continue on the main trail 150 yards beyond the cabin to a fork where a sign points left to Conundrum Hot Springs. Turn left, cross a side stream and climb several yards to the pools.

To reach Triangle Pass continue straight at the junction above the cabin.

Hot springs bath

Horse party near trail head

38 AMERICAN LAKE

One day trip or backpack
Distance: 3.2 miles one way
Elevation gain: 1,970 feet
High point: 11,370 feet
Allow 2 to 2½ hours one way
Usually open July through September
Topographic map:
U.S.G.S. Hayden Peak, Colo.
7.5′   1960

The climb through a fine stand of aspen, across large grassy slopes and beneath tall conifers to the timberline setting of American Lake is the easiest of the four trips in the Ashcroft area (see No's. 37, 39 and 40). Hikers who want a more strenuous trek can explore the basin above the lake or attempt to follow the faint route that heads south from the southeastern shore for 0.5 mile to an old digging. Start the hike with adequate drinking water.

The trailhead is only 1.5 miles north of the townsite of Ashcroft and you may want to stroll among the remains of this mining town that was at its peak from 1880 through 1883 and reached a maximum population of around 1,000. During the late 1880's many of the homes were dragged down the valley to Aspen as that community became the most important mining center in the area.

Drive 0.5 mile west of Aspen on Colorado 82 to a road on the south side of the highway where a sign states Maroon Lake and Ashcroft. Turn south and immediately meet a fork. Keep left and proceed 10 miles to a sign on your right stating American Lake 3 across the road from the Elk Mountain Lodge. Turn right into the large, open area where there is ample parking.

Follow the path that climbs from the parking area and after several yards merge with an old road and level off. Cross a stream that flows under the road and 200 yards from the trailhead come to a fork and veer left, as indicated by the sign pointing to American Lake Trail. Walk up through a narrow little valley of aspen for 0.1 mile then turn right and begin climbing at a steady, moderate grade in three sets of switchbacks of irregular lengths. Interestingly, the north facing side of the valley is forested with conifers but the wall you are climbing is covered with aspen. At 1.0 mile begin a long traverse and after 0.5 mile drop slightly then abruptly enter a zone of evergreens.

Begin hiking at a gradual grade and travel along the lower edge of immense, grassy slopes. A few hundred feet before reentering woods pass a sign marking the obscure Sandy Range Trail. Continue on the level through the forest for a short distance then climb to the crest of a ridge at 2.2 miles. Curve right, descend slightly and begin traversing the south side of the ridge where you can see into the southern end of Castle Creek valley. Hike through an aspen grove, more coniferous woods and some open areas before entering an alpine setting of scree slopes and scattered trees. The squeaks and whistles of conies and marmots are heard frequently in this rocky area. Come to a point just above the lake and walk the few final yards to the shore.

American Lake

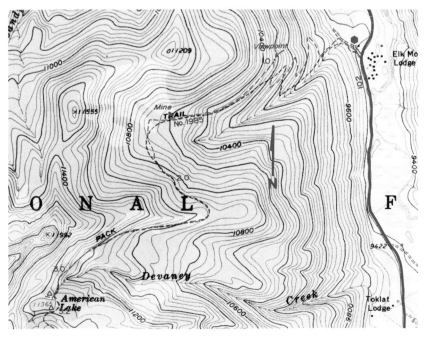

39 CATHEDRAL LAKE

One day trip or backpack
Distance: 3 miles one way
Elevation gain: 2,200 feet
High point: 11,870 feet
Allow 2 hours one way
Usually open July through September
Topographic map:
   U.S.G.S. Hayden Peak, Colo.
   7.5′   **1960**

Emerald-colored Cathedral Lake derives its name from the massive spires that surround it on three sides. The climb through two valleys of varying vegetation to the shore is the second most demanding of the four hikes in the Ashcroft area (see No's. 37, 38 and 40). The route to Cathedral Lake fords Pine Creek three times and, although the crossings are not difficult, they will be easier later in the summer. No drinking water is easily obtainable until 2.4 miles.

Electric Pass is visible from Cathedral Lake and you can reach it by following a rugged hiker's trail for two miles with 1,700 feet of additional climbing. The route then winds down to a junction with the trail to Conundrum Hot Springs (No. 37).

Proceed 0.5 mile west of Aspen on Colorado 82 to a road on the south side of the highway where a sign states Maroon Lake and Ashcroft. Turn south and immediately meet a fork. Keep left and drive 12 miles to a sign stating Cathedral Lake Trail. Turn right and go 0.5 mile to a parking area at the road's end. A sign on the west side of the turnaround stating Cathedral Lake Trail identifies the beginning of the hike.

Climb gradually then moderately through an aspen grove. As you gain elevation the grade increases and conifers become more prominent. At 1.6 miles leave the woods and traverse the north wall of the lower valley at a more gradual grade. A boisterous stretch of Pine Creek tumbles down the gorge below to your left. At one point you can see a digging in the sheer rock wall of the defile. Make one set of short switchbacks, pass through a clump of woods and switchback twice more. Make a third set of short switchbacks at 1.5 miles just before coming to the notch at the head of the lower valley.

Walk at a gradual grade for several hundred feet, keep left at a fork and drop slightly. Resume climbing moderately and travel above a marshy meadow, divided by a placid, meandering section of Pine Creek. Pass through a rocky area where you probably will hear the squeaks of conies, descend gradually and ford Pine Creek.

Climb along a slope of trees, brush and rocks in several switchbacks. Pass the remains of a cabin on your left then recross Pine Creek at a notch. Turn sharply left and continue up through bushes and trees for 200 yards to a campground with a picnic table and outhouse. Climb along the trail from the campsites for 50 yards to a junction and a sign that lists mileages to Electric Pass and Conundrum Trail.

To reach Cathedral Lake keep left and go through bushes for a few yards to the third ford of Pine Creek. Wind up across irregular terrain of grass, scattered rocks and stunted trees for 400 yards to the shore of the lake.

Cathedral Peak

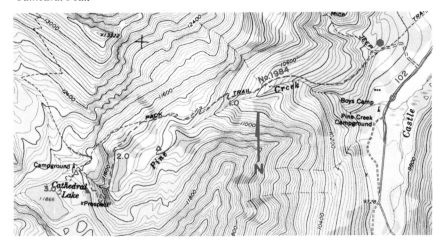

40 PEARL PASS

One day trip
Distance: 5.7 miles one way
Elevation gain: 2,955 feet
High point: 12,705 feet
Allow 3½ to 4 hours one way
Usually open July through September
Topographic maps:
    U.S.G.S. Hayden Peak, Colo.
    7.5′   1960
    U.S.G.S. Pearl Pass, Colo.
    7.5′   1961

The road between Crested Butte and Ashcroft over Pearl Pass was opened in 1882 and stagecoaches and pack trains carrying coal soon were regular users of the route. However, when the railroad reached the growing town of Aspen in 1887 a considerably more efficient method of transporting the coal was available and the Pearl Pass route was abandoned. This hike follows the old track through exceptionally delightful scenery. The second half of the trip winds above timberline over uneven terrain of grass, rocks and tarns with bright accents of color added by the blossoms of Indian paintbrush, alpine sunflowers, brook primroses, phlox and other wild flowers.

Drive 0.5 mile west of Aspen on Colorado 82 to a road on the south side of the highway where a sign states Maroon Lake and Ashcroft. Turn south and immediately meet a fork. Keep left and proceed 13 miles to a fork, a short distance beyond where the pavement ends. Keep right, following the sign to Montezuma Basin. Unless you have a 4-wheel drive vehicle you probably will want to park your car off the road after about 0.7 mile.

Walk along the road at a gentle grade through woods and open areas. Curve above a large pond and at 0.9 mile cross Castle Creek on a bridge. Continue up along the road and near 2.4 miles pass above a cabin. Mining debris and machinery can be seen across the creek. One-tenth mile farther cross Castle Creek on a second bridge, wind up in a few short switchbacks and come to the junction of the road to Montezuma Basin.

Turn left and continue up a road. From here to Pearl Pass you will pass a few areas populated by conies. One-tenth mile from the junction come to the third crossing of Castle Creek. Go up to the right a few yards and cross the flow on a small dam. The steep-roofed cabin above you is used in winter by cross-country skiers. Climb along the rocky road and soon come to timberline. Begin winding up over the hummocks of grass, rocks and low-growing vegetation. Along this section you can see into barren Montezuma Basin to the north. The famous H.A.W. Tabor was part owner of the Montezuma Mine that, generally, was not a profitable venture. Pass a tarn, then another one just before a broad crest at 4.0 miles. From here you can see Pearl Pass on the rim of the basin to the southeast and the route of the road to it.

Descend slightly along the grassy hillside, crossing a broad, shallow side stream then resume climbing gradually. In contrast to the usual abandoned mines encountered on hikes throughout the Rockies you can look east across the valley to the ribbons of roads servicing a large, active iron mine. Enter a basin of huge boulders and cross the rocks on the road whose surface, fortunately, is considerably smoother than the surrounding terrain. Traverse up the basin wall for the final 0.2 mile to the pass. You can see east to the Gore Range and southeast as far as the San Juans. Pearl Pass is the most southerly destination of this guide.

Pinnacles west of the pass

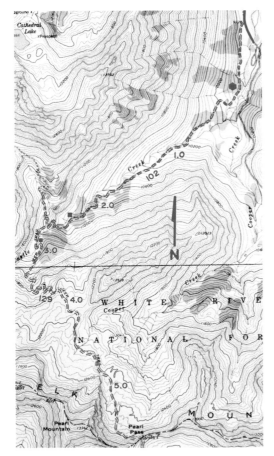

41 MIDWAY PASS TRAIL

One day trip or backpack
Distance: 2.3 miles one way
Elevation gain: 1,520 feet
High point: 12,000 feet
Allow 2 hours one way
Usually open late June through September
Topographic maps:
    U.S.G.S. Independence Pass, Colo.
    7.5'   **1960**
    U.S.G.S. Mt. Champion, Colo.
    7.5'   **1960**
    U.S.G.S. New York Peak, Colo.
    7.5'   **1960**
    U.S.G.S. Thimble Rock, Colo.
    7.5'   **1960**

Five hikes described in this guide begin at or a short distance west of Independence Pass: the trails to South Fork Pass (No. 42) and Lost Man Lake (No. 43) travel along grassy valley bottoms for most of their distances. Number 44, to the mines of Independence, begins at the remains of a ghost town and traverses up to more buildings and diggings. The path from Independence Pass along a ridge crest to Peak 13,020 (No. 45) offers extensive views of the central Colorado Rockies. These scenic, enjoyable trips are only two to three miles long, except for the one to South Fork Pass that is 4.3 miles, and the grades are gradual to moderate.

The hike along the Midway Pass Trail is described only to a cluster of tarns perched high above timberline on a rolling, grassy slope. The view from this lovely spot includes landmarks in the Maroon Bells-Snowmass and Lincoln Creek areas. However, you can continue along the trail for one additional mile with 100 feet of elevation gain to Midway Pass where trails head both north and south.

Proceed on Colorado 82 15 miles east of Aspen or six miles west of Independence Pass to a sign on the north side of the road stating Independence Trail. This marker is just west of a small highway bridge and 200 yards west of the entrance to Lost Man Campground. A large turnout is off the south side of the highway across from the trailhead.

Walk through woods for a few hundred yards to a clearing and the junction of a faint path to the South Fork Pass Trail. Keep straight (left) and begin climbing in many switchbacks along the wooded slope. As the trail rises the aspen gradually are replaced by pines. However, the woods are open and do not obstruct the view down onto Lost Man Reservoir and the broad valley beyond it.

At 1.1 miles make the last switchback and come to a bench. Walk past a rock wall and small boulder field then climb for a short distance to a brushy clearing. During this latter section you can look south beyond the long ridge with Green Mountain (see No. 44) as its high point to Grizzly Peak (see No. 50) and Peak 13,020. Enter a woods of large conifers then curve slightly north and climb through more sparse timber. At 1.8 miles come to timberline and traverse gradually west along the gentle, grassy slope. Cairns and tall stakes mark the route where the tread is faint. Cross several small side streams and 0.5 mile from the edge of the woods hike just above the large tarn that makes a good stopping place or campsite.

Old stove near the tarns

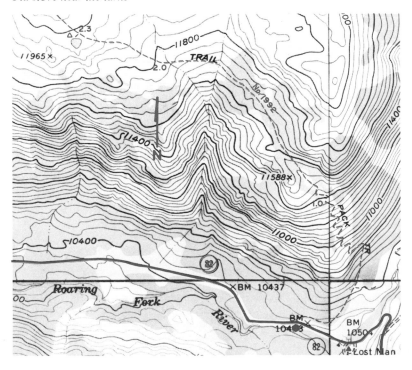

42 SOUTH FORK PASS

One day trip
Distance: 4.3 miles one way
Elevation gain: 1,150 feet
High point: 11,750 feet
Allow 2 hours one way
Usually open late June through September
Topographic map:
U.S.G.S. Mt. Champion, Colo.
7.5′   1960

The trail up the length of the broad valley of Lost Man Creek to grassy South Fork Pass is the longest of this guide's five hikes in the Independence Pass area. Those wanting a slightly longer trip can continue 1.5 miles beyond the Pass with 800 feet of elevation loss to small Deadman Lake and more explorative hikers can attempt to follow the faint route that heads east from the 4.1 mile point to Lost Man Lake (No. 43).

Drive on Colorado 82 six miles west of Independence Pass or 15 miles east of Aspen to an unpaved road on the north side of the highway marked by a sign stating Lost Man Trail and Reservoir. Turn north, follow the spur to above the small reservoir and park your car.

(You can follow the old road north along the east side of Lost Man Creek but you will have to ford the heavy flow near 1.9 miles. If you choose this route, bear left after crossing a side stream at 1.4 miles and intercept a lower road. Keep right where any spurs go left and at the ford continue upstream several yards for a better crossing point. During the walk along the road you can look across the valley floor to the main trail.)

To follow the official route drop to the dam across the reservoir, cross on it and turn right. Walk at a gradual grade along the generally grassy floor. As you progress up the valley you will pass the usual array of charming wild flowers, including columbine, Indian paintbrush, elephant heads and bottle brush. Near 1.4 miles enter a stand of timber and farther on hop across a stream identified as Jack Creek.

Continue in woods for a short distance then resume traveling along more open terrain and come to the point where the road along the east side of the valley floor joins the official route. Keep climbing, cross a side stream and where the trail forks you can follow either branch. Climb more noticeably for a short distance then resume a gradual grade. Hop a somewhat larger side stream then climb moderately to the south end of the South Fork Pass area and walk through the grassy little vale to its north end. The jagged peaks across the valley to the northwest are the southern tip of the Williams Mountains. If no thunderstorms are threatening, a good side trip is the easy climb of the 12,825 foot peak to the east of South Fork Pass.

94

Late spring snow

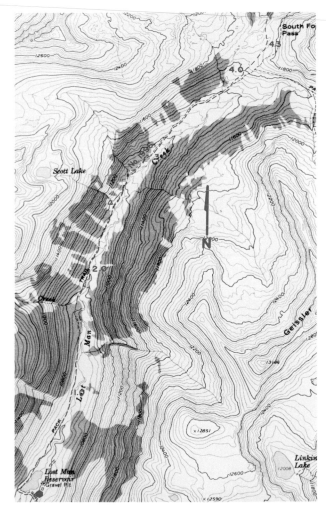

43 LOST MAN LAKE

One day trip or backpack
Distance: 3 miles one way
Elevation gain: 1,320 feet; loss 350 feet
High point: 12,820 feet
Allow 1½ to 2½ hours one way
Usually open July through mid-September
Topographic map:
    U.S.G.S. Mt. Champion, Colo.
    7.5′   1960

This hike is the only one of the five hikes in the Independence Pass area that visits a sizeable lake — in fact, two of them. The route, that is above timberline for the entire distance, climbs through a broad, grassy valley beside a lively stream to Independence Lake then goes over a small pass and winds down to Lost Man Lake. You can save the 350 feet of elevation loss and shorten the trip by a total of 1.2 miles by ending the hike at the saddle between the two lakes.

Drive on Colorado 82 two miles northwest of Independence Pass or 19 miles east of Aspen to a sign on the north side of the highway identifying the beginning of the Lost Man Lake Trail. Parking for a few cars is available along the shoulder.

Climb gradually along the valley floor near the Roaring Fork River, passing clusters of bushes and crossing many small side streams. After 0.5 mile begin climbing more noticeably and at 1.1 miles come to the edge of a large basin where the tread stops. Cross the floor of the bowl, generally heading toward the main creek that flows down the center of the northeastern wall. Portions of the basin are swampy but you will be able to circumvent most of the wet areas. Begin climbing the wall and as you near the top you can turn around and look southwest to Linkins Lake on a bench 500 feet above the beginning of the hike. You could make a cross-country side trip to this lake on the return if you wanted a more challenging trek.

At the top of the basin wall level off and pass near the end of Independence Lake. Walk parallel to its northwestern shore then climb gradually for one-third mile to the low saddle north of the lake. Although you may locate portions of a faint path on the return, you probably will be traveling cross-country beyond the 1.1 mile point to just below the saddle. However, the route always is obvious and the terrain presents no problems.

From the saddle you will be able to look back down to Independence Lake and beyond to rugged peaks and north over Lost Man Lake to the Williams Mountains. If you plan to visit Lost Man Lake follow the faint path that begins winding down from the saddle just to the east of where the trail from Independence Lake reached the crest.

Lost Man Lake

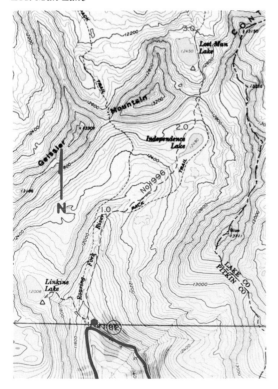

44 MINES OF INDEPENDENCE

One day trip
Distance: 2 miles one way
Elevation gain: 780 feet
High point: 11,600 feet
Allow 1 to 1½ hours one way
Usually open mid-June through September
Topographic maps:
 U.S.G.S. Independence Pass, Colo.
 7.5' 1960
 U.S.G.S. New York Peak, Colo.
 7.5' 1960

On the 4th of July, 1879 a gold strike was made a few miles west of Hunters (later renamed Independence) Pass and the four main mining camps that quickly appeared soon merged into a single community. Aptly, the town was named Independence and reached its peak in the mid-1880's when the population was around 2,000. The community was a stage station and the western terminus of the toll road over the pass to Twin Lakes. During the late 1880's Independence's population declined when the mining activity shifted to Aspen. Today, ruins beside the highway and scattered along the valley below mark the site of the ghost town.

The route of this hike follows an old road along the south wall of the valley to more remains and diggings. If you want a longer trip you can continue an additional three-quarters mile with 300 feet of elevation gain to a broad, grassy pass at the north edge of the Lincoln Creek drainage. From this crest you could continue west up along the ridge to the summit of 12,791-foot Green Mountain. The stream crossing at the beginning of the hike is more easily negotiated later in the summer.

Drive on Colorado 82 4.5 miles west of Independence Pass or 16.5 miles east of Aspen to the most westerly of the ruins of Independence above and below the highway. A few parking spaces are available along a broad section of the shoulder.

Walk down an old road to the creek and go upstream through bushes for several yards to where some planks may be placed across the flow. Traverse up to the west along the road and cross a small side stream. Since you are traveling at 11,000 feet you probably will appreciate the moderate grade of the road. Enter a stand of conifers and pass above the ruins of a cabin.

At 0.7 mile go in and out of a little side canyon then begin switchbacking. During the climb you can see across the highway to Lost Man Reservoir and the long, broad valley extending behind it. The trail to South Fork Pass (No. 42) traverses the length of this valley floor. Another view is east beyond the remains of Independence to Peak 13,020 (No. 45).

Pass below a cabin after the first turn and continue winding up to a large log cabin and a smaller metal building. The road that heads southwest across the slope just before you reach the cabin goes to the caved-in shaft of a big digging. Continue along the road that heads northwest beyond the log cabin. Enter woods, curve left then right, passing more ruins, and come to a large, very swampy meadow. More cabins are along the north end of the clearing.

To reach the pass, turn sharply left at the edge of the meadow, staying on its east side, and follow the old jeep tracks for 50 yards then turn right and climb to power lines. Follow them, traveling just downslope from the lines, across the grass to the pass. The summit of Green Mountain is ¾ mile to the west and 800 feet higher.

Old log cabin near the mine tunnels

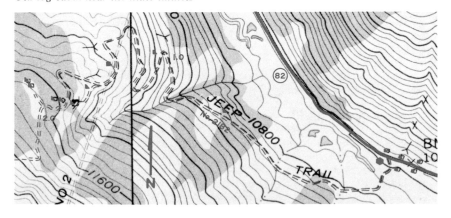

45 PEAK 13,020

One-half day trip
Distance: 2.4 miles one way
Elevation gain: 1,060 feet; loss 140 feet
High point: 13,020 feet
Allow 1½ to 2 hours one way
Usually open July through mid-September
Topographic map:
   U.S.G.S. Independence Pass, Colo.
   7.5′   1960

Of the many scenic passes in Colorado crossed by roads, 12,093-foot Independence Pass is one of the most spectacular. This hike begins from a nature trail at the pass and follows the treeless crest of the Continental Divide to the summit of Peak 13,020 (the elevation of the unnamed high point) where the impressive view extends west as far as the Snowmass area.

Although the grade alway is gradual and most of the route follows an obvious use-path, you will be traveling between 12,000 and 13,000 feet above sea level so the hike may be more demanding than the distance and elevation gain might indicate. Since the trip is along an open, high ridge crest for

the entire distance, do not start or continue if a thunderstorm is building.

If you feel like a second trip you can make the three mile hike to Lost Man Lake (No. 43) that begins just two miles north of Independence Pass.

Drive on Colorado 82 to the large parking area at Independence Pass located 21 miles east of Aspen and 17 miles west of Twin Lakes.

Walk into the observation area where a signed, short nature trail affords an informative side trip before or after the hike. Look west for a two-rut road that wanders up near the crest and follow it. One mile from the highway drop slightly then resume climbing to the string of high metal fences along the crest. These barricades have been placed to create greater accumulations of snow. In the summer, when the usual cover has melted and run off, these drifts still will be melting, thus providing a more protracted supply of water for the valley reservoirs. Although you can hike on either side of the fences, a path parallels the east side of the structures and offers an unobstructed view of Mountain Boy Gulch.

At the south end of the wall of fences descend along the crest, losing about 100 feet of elevation, then resume climbing and follow a faint path for 0.5 mile to a cluster of rocky outcroppings. Scramble up through the boulders along their right (west) side. The final 0.5 mile to the summit of Peak 13,020 is over talus that resembles a slope of stone dinner plates. You will be following a path for most of this stretch.

During your stay on the summit you can study leisurely the scenery you enjoyed along the climb: Mountain Boy Gulch and Independence Pass and the peaks directly above it are to the northeast. Across the deep valley to the south is the impressive, snow-covered face of Grizzly Peak. A trail (No. 50) traverses the length of the valley and ends at Grizzly Lake nestled at the base of the mountain. The lake is hidden from view behind an immense rock outcropping but if you have visited the large tarn you easily will be able to identify its location. Snowmass Mountain is the two-horned summit on the western horizon.

Because of the steep, unstable terrain, attempting to reach the broad summit to the east is not a good side trip.

Looking south from Independence Pass

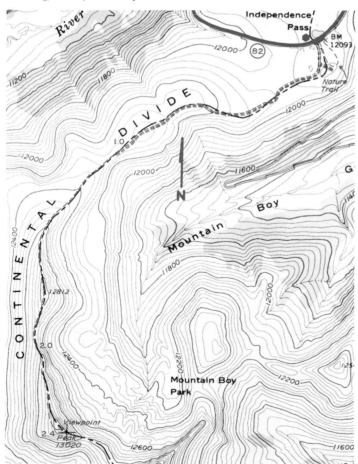

46 NEW YORK CREEK TRAIL

One day trip or backpack
Distance: 4.4 miles one way
Elevation gain: 2,165 feet
High point: 12,265 feet
Allow 2½ to 3 hours one way
Usually open July through September
Topographic map:
   U.S.G.S. New York Peak, Colo.
   7.5′   1960

The final five trails in this guide traverse slopes of the Lincoln Creek drainage, situated between Independence Pass and Aspen. Each of the hikes, all moderately difficult, travels through valleys of varying sizes and character and end at or near lakes well above timberline. The terrain beyond the end of the Tabor Creek Trail (No. 47) is especially good for exploring and the steep climb to Truro Lake (No. 48) involves some route finding. On the hike to Petroleum Lake (No. 49) you pass cabins, a waterwheel and other mining remains and you could make a side trip to the ghost town of Ruby. Other evidences of past mining activity in the form of diggings and a tunnel are beside the route to Grizzly Lake (No. 50) at the base of imposing Grizzly Peak.

All hikes, except to Petroleum Lake, involve fording large streams so these trips are best done after at least mid-July.

A good spot to end the hike along the New York Creek Trail is on the unnamed pass at 4.4 miles but if you want to go farther, a trail does continue west toward Ashcroft. Cross-country excursions can be made to some unnamed lakes 0.6 mile from the main route and southeast from the pass across open slopes for 2.0 miles to Ptarmigan (Tellurium on U.S.G.S. maps) Lake.

Drive on Colorado 82 to a sign identifying Lincoln Creek Road 10 miles west of Independence Pass and 11 miles east of Aspen. Turn south, after 0.5 mile keep left at the entrance to Lincoln Gulch Campground and travel three miles to a sign on the right stating New York Creek Trail at a side road. Although narrow and unpaved, Lincoln Creek Road is not especially rough or steep. Parking spaces are available along the shoulder or off the spur road.

Walk along the side road for 150 yards to the ford of Lincoln Creek then follow the road up across an open slope and through woods for 1.0 mile to the canal maintenance road. Turn right, hike at a gradual grade for 0.5 mile and pass the stream flowing from Brooklyn Gulch. Continue on the road around the end of a small ridge and a few yards before the road ends at a diversion dam on New York Creek look for a sign stating New York Creek Trail on the bank above you.

Turn left, leaving the road, and climb gradually through woods. Soon you will be traveling above patches of meadow on the valley floor. At 2.3 miles drop slightly and cross New York Creek. Because of possible contamination from grazing, obtain your drinking water from side streams only. Climb more noticeably along a grassy slope then traverse through a finger of woods. Resume hiking along an open slope and cross a side stream, a good place for a snack stop. Continue along the grassy valley wall, make one set of short switchbacks, cross another small side stream and after a few hundred feet reenter dense timber at 3.0 miles.

After 0.3 mile the huge conifers thin out and the trail crosses a stream near a good campsite. Continue up through the open woods, switchback once and climb to timberline at a crest. During your hike up the valley you could see the pass and from this crest it is especially easy to identify. Follow the tall stakes across the tundra, cross a side stream—the last source of water—and follow the path up to the pass. Just before the last pitch you can look left to the lakes at the head of the valley that make a good cross-country side trip.

Hiker at the pass

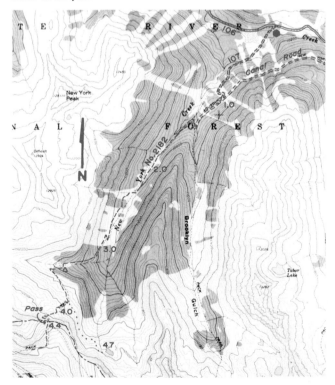

47 TABOR CREEK TRAIL

One day trip or backpack
Distance: 2.8 miles one way
Elevation gain: 1,900 feet
High point: 12,120 feet
Allow 3 hours one way
Usually open July through September
Topographic map:
    U.S.G.S. New York Peak, Colo.
    7.5′   1960

beginning of the hike, plan to do the trip later in the season, preferably after mid-July. However, you can avoid the ford by driving two miles farther along the main road to the dam across Grizzly Reservoir. Walk across the dam, turn right and climb very gradually along the canal maintenance road for 2.0 miles to a bridge over the canal.

Proceed on Colorado 82 to a sign identifying Lincoln Creek Road located 10 miles west of Independence Pass and 11 miles east of Aspen. Turn south, after 0.5 mile keep left at the entrance to Lincoln Gulch Campground and travel four miles to a sign on your right stating Tabor Creek Trail. Although unpaved and narrow, the road is not especially rough or steep. Parking is available off the road.

Walk southeast down a faint road for 200 feet to the ford of Lincoln Creek. From the south bank wind up through woods for 0.2 mile to the canal maintenance road. Cross the canal on a bridge and resume climbing for a short distance to the ford of Tabor Creek. Continue south up through woods for several hundred yards to the edge of the timber then begin traversing along the western wall of the large valley. The trail is faint near timberline but soon becomes obvious as it travels along the grassy slope. If you have difficulty relocating the route traverse south high enough above the valley floor that you are not in the ravine formed by Tabor Creek.

Where the trail becomes obscure again continue traversing to the south. The floor of this valley is more irregular than most and the route climbs through a few little grassy basins. Near 2.4 miles curve slightly southeast and climb the low, but steeper, slope just below the unnamed lake. Although this stretch presents no technical problems, you may need to retrace your steps to locate the best route around the scattered outcroppings.

Although a good stopping place for this hike is the alpine setting of the unnamed lake at 2.8 miles, you can continue up the grassy valley to a low pass and descend slightly to a shallow lake sprawled in a large tundra basin. The climb to the saddle would add a total of 0.8 mile and 600 feet of elevation gain and the drop to the lake would add another 0.2 mile and 150 feet of climbing on the return.

Much of the route beyond 1.0 mile is faint or non-existent but you should have no trouble reaching your destination. Since you will be fording Lincoln Creek at the

If you want to explore the route beyond the lake curve into the little valley southwest of the tarn. Follow the path along the eastern wall, traveling above some tarns below to the right. Enter a large basin and traverse south along its western wall. Climb to a sloping bench then wind up the final distance to the pass where you can look down on the shallow lake in the basin to the south.

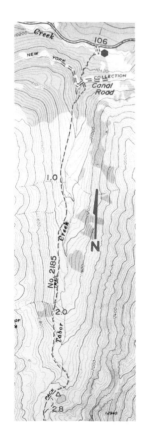

Tabor Creek Canyon

105

48 TRURO LAKE

One day trip or backpack
Distance: 3 miles one way
Elevation gain: 1,590 feet
High point: 12,180 feet
Allow 2½ to 3 hours one way
Usually open July through September
Topographic maps:
    U.S.G.S. Independence Pass, Colo.
    7.5'   1960
    U.S.G.S. New York Peak, Colo.
    7.5'   1960

Many hikes described in this guide end at lakes situated in massive basins that beg for exploration but answering that call usually demands more time and energy than is available. The little valley that holds Truro Lake is a manageable exception. However, reaching the valley floor does involve one mile of generally cross-country travel up a steep, wooded slope. Because of the ford of Lincoln Creek, the trip is best done after mid-July.

Drive on Colorado 82 to a sign identifying Lincoln Creek Road located 10 miles west of Independence Pass and 11 miles east of Aspen. Turn south, after 0.5 mile keep left at the entrance to Lincoln Gulch Campground and travel six miles to the dam at the north end of Grizzly Reservoir. Although unpaved and narrow, the road is not especially rough or steep. Keep left and drive above the reservoir maintenance buildings. Go 0.1 mile to the entrance to Portal Campground. Turn right into the small parking area.

Walk south on the almost level jeep road along the grassy valley floor, periodically passing through fingers of timber. During the first part of the hike you can see beaver dams and the resultant ponds along sections of Lincoln Creek. At 1.3 miles pass the remains of a corral and come to a fork in the road at a huge boulder. Follow the right branch for several yards then turn sharply right and walk downhill along a faint, grassy roadbed to a small campsite on your left. Ford Lincoln Creek a few feet downstream on some rocks. After the crossing turn left and walk to the southwest across an open area.

Where you come near Truro Creek turn right and begin climbing steeply. You probably will not be able to locate a tread. Climb generally parallel to, but not necessarily beside, Truro Creek as, periodically, the best route may be as much as a few hundred feet from the stream. However, the route never crosses the flow. As you climb higher you probably will be on portions of the faint trail. Come close to Truro Creek and travel beside it for a short distance.

Near timberline the grade becomes gentle and the trail passes the remains of a log cabin. As frequently occurs in the Colorado Rockies, the vegetation changes abruptly from deep woods to grassy slopes. Walk along the floor of the narrow valley, bearing slightly left (south). Pass a long tarn in a rocky setting at the base of Truro Peak then curve left and begin climbing toward the head of the valley. As you rise the terrain becomes increasingly rocky but you will be able to continue on the grass, unless you prefer traveling over rougher terrain. One hundred yards before the lake walk through a big gulley of boulders and come to the northern shore. No adequate campsites are at or near Truro Lake.

Truro Lake

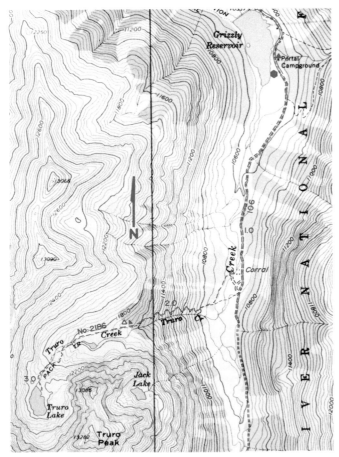

49 PETROLEUM LAKE

One day trip or backpack
Distance: 5.3 miles one way
Elevation gain: 1,750 feet
High point: 12,300 feet
Allow 3 hours one way
Usually open July through September
Topographic maps:
    U.S.G.S. Independence Pass, Colo.
    7.5′   1960
    U.S.G.S. New York Peak, Colo.
    7.5′   1960

The expanse of tundra surrounding Petroleum Lake and the rocky, barren wall of peaks above to the west create an impressive and stark setting. In contrast to this arctic-like scene, the first four miles of the hike are along the grassy floor of broad Lincoln Creek Valley or through woods. The jeep road the hike follows for most of the distance passes various remains of past mining activity and you could make a short side trip to the abandoned mining town of Ruby.

Proceed on Colorado 82 to a sign identifying Lincoln Creek Road located 10 miles west of Independence Pass and 11 miles east of Aspen. Turn south, after 0.5 mile keep left at the entrance to Lincoln Gulch Campground and travel six miles to the dam at the north end of Grizzly Reservoir. Although narrow and unpaved, the road is not especially rough or steep. Keep left, drive above the reservoir maintenance buildings and continue 0.1 mile to the entrance to Portal Campground. Turn right and leave your car in the small parking area near the lake.

Walk south on the almost level jeep road along the grassy valley floor, periodically passing through fingers of timber. At 1.3 miles pass the remains of a corral and a short distance farther come to a fork. Follow either branch and continue along the road. Near 2.0 miles begin climbing more noticeably. The summit of the ridge above to the east is Grizzly Peak. This side is much less impressive than the steep north face that rises from the shore of Grizzly Lake (No. 50).

At 2.9 miles pass an old cabin on your left. Rubble beyond the building indicates this was the site of a sawmill. The remains of a water wheel are just above the creek several hundred feet back down the road. Where a faint side route goes downhill toward a cabin across the creek continue climbing along the main road. About 0.3 mile beyond the mill site come to the junction of a more obvious roadbed. The main road continues straight for three-quarters mile to the site of Ruby.

Turn right and descend to Lincoln Creek. Cross the stream on a decrepit bridge. Pass the ruins of a cabin and begin winding steeply up the wooded slope. From here you can look south up the valley to the remaining buildings of Ruby. Pass a rustic residence and 0.2 mile farther pass a dilapidated cabin on your left and beyond it a cozy abandoned cabin adjacent to the north side of the road. Continue uphill and after several hundred yards come to timberline. Climb along the brushy slope then level off and come to a fork. To reach the northern shore of Anderson Lake continue straight for 150 feet.

Turn right and drop slightly along the road. You can continue along the road to Petroleum Lake or take a cross-country route. If you decide on the latter, veer left where the road resumes climbing and head uphill, aiming for the right (east) base of the large rock outcropping above. During the ascent you can turn around for an overview of Anderson Lake. At the crest of the grassy slope bear very slightly left and continue at a gradual grade for the remaining few hundred yards to the shore of Petroleum Lake. If you are following the road, walk at a gradual grade and pass a large tarn. Climb very steeply for a few hundred feet just before reaching the lake. A path goes to a digging above the north side.

Petroleum Lake

Old sawmill water wheel

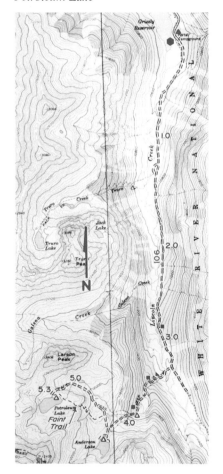

50 GRIZZLY LAKE

One day trip or backpack
Distance: 3.1 miles one way
Elevation gain: 1,960 feet
High point: 12,550 feet
Allow 2½ to 3 hours one way
Usually open July through September
Topographic map:
  U.S.G.S. Independence Pass, Colo.
  7.5′   1960

The steep northern face of Grizzly Peak looms over Grizzly Lake and from a comfortable spot on the tundra surrounding the shore you can look across the water and mentally climb to the summit. An old mining tunnel is visible from the main trail below the lake and if you want to examine the excavation you can follow a path to its entrance. After mid-July the ford of Grizzly Creek presents no problems; before then the flow may be heavy.

Drive on Colorado 82 to a sign identifying Lincoln Creek Road located 10 miles west of Independence Pass and 11 miles east of Aspen. Turn south, after 0.5 mile keep left at the entrance to Lincoln Gulch Campground and travel six miles to the dam at the north end of Grizzly Reservoir. Although unpaved and narrow, the road is not especially rough or steep. Keep left and drive above the reservoir maintenance buildings. One-tenth mile from the dam and 200 feet before crossing Grizzly Creek pass the beginning of a trail heading east from the road. Although the trail is obvious for its entire distance, its beginning is not marked by an official sign. Drive a short distance farther to the entrance to Portal Campground, turn right and leave your car in the small parking area by the lake.

Retrace your route along the road to the trailhead and soon begin winding up through woods at a moderate grade. Be sure to stay on the official route—short-cutting disrupts the drainage patterns and causes erosion gulleys. At 0.4 mile leave the woods and come to the western end of a broad, grassy valley. Traverse at a gradual grade, occasionally passing through small stands of timber. Travel below some interesting outcroppings then at 1.0 mile, after crossing a rocky, usually dry stream bed, stay on the left and higher trail. The crest of the slope to the left is the Continental Divide and the high point on the ridge directly above you at the 1.0 mile point is the destination of the hike from Independence Pass to Peak 13,020 (No. 45).

Enter the final grove of trees at 1.8 miles and near its southern end pass the remains of a cabin on your left just upslope from the trail. Keep right at the junction of the faint route that climbs along the valley wall past Ouray Peak to McNasser Gulch and continue traversing the grassy slope for a short distance. Curve right and drop slightly to the ford of Grizzly Creek and resume traversing.

The valley becomes considerably narrower and the trail grade steeper. As the route curves to the southwest you will have a view of the impressive north face of Grizzly Peak. Pass diggings on your right and continue up to a small bench of grass, boulders and tarns. Resume climbing and after about 150 yards come to a large cairn in the middle of the path.

Turn left and follow more cairns through a grass swale. Although the route is faint here, you can see the obvious trail traversing up the slope ahead to the west. Begin walking on a defined tread and continue to the base of the slope. Turn sharply left and begin climbing above the tarn-dotted bench. Watch for rock fall along this stretch. From here you can see the tunnel in the outcropping to the south and the path leading to its entrance. At the end of the rocky stretch traverse over tundra for a few hundred feet to the northeastern end of the lake. The one campsite here is not protected from winds.

Abandoned mine shaft near the lake

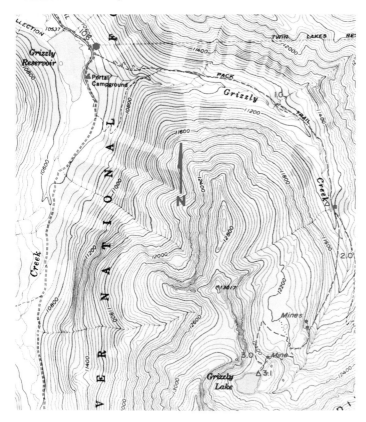

Cover Photo
  Missouri Lakes

Editor
  Thomas K. Worcester

Cover Design
  Dean McMullen